Praise for *Kings and Queens in the Kingdom of God*

"Irenaeus of Lyon, the great second-century theologian, is famous for his attempt to express the essence of Christianity with the pithy adage, "the glory of God is a human being fully alive." Keith White's *Kings and Queens in the Kingdom of God* is a contemporary call to return to this timeless truth that is at the very heart of the gospel of our Lord Jesus Christ. In a world that is growing darker every day, I pray that this little book will be used to remind all faithful Christ-followers that there is no higher calling in life than to "let your light shine before others, that they may see your good deeds and glorify your Father in heaven" (Mt 5:16)."
David O. Williams, D.Min, Lead Superintendent of EFC-MAYM, Interim Director of EFC-International

"*Kings and Queens in the Kingdom of God* is a biblically informed and wide-ranging treatise on how every believer can find fulfillment in his or her God-given purpose and role in the Kingdom of God. By following along with Keith's well-thought-out tracing of creating order, meaning, purpose, and value, beginning at creation, we can gain much-needed insight into our own unique contribution to God's Kingdom rather than focusing our energy on trying to build our own kingdoms."
Dr. Robert E. Logan, author of The Discipleship Difference and An Undivided Heart

"As we can clearly see all the beauty God has created in cultural diversity, we can also see the Godly principles intended to cross all human beings. This book is an expression of that endeavor we must come to terms with in order to grow closer to God to know better who we are and ultimately, who He is."
Daniel Kramer, Associate VP of Global Programs and Partnerships and Dean of the Institute of Biblical Translation at Barclay College

"I recommend reading *Kings and Queens in the Kingdom of God* to see your life's purpose is to "have dominion" in your sphere of influence (Gen. 1:28). As a measure of my progress in doing so, I have begun reflecting on the following questions at the end of Chapter 6: "What does Jesus mean to you? What do you think you mean to Jesus?"
Clark Pickett

"I enjoyed this treatise on our real purpose in life. Now I understand better why I continually strive for order in my farming operation."
Elmer Davis, local large farmer

"Wow! I just finished reading *Kings and Queens in the Kingdom of God*, and I am personally challenged to align my own life to the destiny God has for me. If you want to understand or clarify your purpose and meaning in life, this book is for you! The biblical, inspiring, and holistic framework that Dr. White, one of my early mentors, lays out here will help the new believer - as well as the rest of us - glorify God in how we live our lives!"
Mike Jordahl, Sr. Vice President of The Navigators

Kings and Queens in the Kingdom of God

Keith White, Ph.D.

Barclay College Publishers

Kings and Queens in the Kingdom of God
Copyright © 2021 by Keith White, Ph.D.

This title is also available as an eBook.
Requests for information should be addressed to:
Barclay College Publishers, 607 N. Kingman St, Haviland, KS 67059

Library of Congress Control Number: 2022931301
Paperback ISBN: 978-1-7354646-1-9
E-book ISBN: 978-1-7354646-2-6

All rights reserved. Published by Barclay College Publishers. No part of this book may be reproduced or transmitted in any form or by any means, electronic or mechanical, including photocopying, recording, or by an information storage and retrieval system—other than for "fair use" as brief quotations embodied in articles and reviews—without written permission from the publisher.

First Printing April 2022
Printed in the United States of America

To Dolores Hope White, my first wife of 44 years, who patiently supported my journey of writing this book but did not get to see it completed.

Table of Contents

Definitions of Terms iii
Introduction v
Chapter One: What is Wrong? 1
Chapter Two: Becoming Kings and Queens 23

The Biblical Evidence

Chapter Three: What's Your Story? 33
Chapter Four: King Adam Before and After His Fall 57
Chapter Five: How God Rules the Fallen God-like 77
Rulers
Chapter Six: Jesus, Our Model Ruler 97

The Psychological Evidence

Chapter Seven: Hard-Wired to Separate 107
Chapter Eight: Drawn to Fill 125

Application

Chapter Nine: Take Your Rightful Throne 141
Chapter Ten: Rule in Harmony With Others 159
Chapter Eleven: Rule with Christ to Build 171
the Kingdom of God

Epilogue 185
Appendix A: Coaching Questions to Help You Discover . . . 193
Your Realm
Appendix B: A Guide for God-like Ruling in a Particular . . . 200
Situation
Acknowledgments 213
About the Author 214

Definitions of Terms

(For the purpose of clarification, the important terms have been defined)

Chaos– Chaos is the state of being contrary to God's purpose. A circumstance can be very orderly, but if it is still not aligned with God's design or does not yet fulfill all of God's purpose to reveal His glory, it is still chaotic. That's because our God is a God of order (1 Corinthians 14:33) who fills everything in every way (e.g. with meaning, purpose, and value [Ephesians 1:23]).

Meaning– Two types of meaning are addressed in this book: spatial meaning and functional meaning. Spatial meaning can refer to a physical relationship of distance and direction between two objects. For instance, item A is six inches to the east of item B, or perhaps item A is in item B. Spatial meaning can also refer to the level of emotional attachment. For instance, Tom means more to Sue than to Sharon because Tom and Sue have been close friends for years, while Sharon hardly knows him. Functional meaning refers to the advantage that A provides B to accomplish one of B's objectives. For instance, Ed's letter of recommendation means a lot to George because it increases George's probability of getting the job.

Purpose– God had a purpose for creating the universe. His purpose is to display His glory. Part of His glory is revealed by the creation of a God-like ruler whom He commanded to rule over His environment for the glory of God. In rebellion, humans often assume they are free to generate a purpose for themselves. Part of God-like ruling is creating purpose in one's environment; however, it is limited to the boundary of what is in alignment with God's character and will glorify him.

Rule– (Hebrew: *radah*) To rule initially meant to subdue and fill God's creation, but after the fall of humanity into sin, the concept of ruling became to subdue other people. God-like ruling begins with separating things to create order and then filling the new order with meaning, purpose, and value, all for the praise of God's glory. God-like ruling also submits to the sovereignty of God by ruling over only the realms that have been given by God.

Subdue– (Hebrew: *kabash*) Given that we were designed to rule over our environment rather than rule over each other, while submitting to God's rule over us, to subdue means to create order out of the chaos. This involves analyzing the thing or situation and affecting the changes necessary to bring it in alignment with God's purpose for it.

Introduction

My dad was a Christian, but he wasn't impressed by the pastors he knew. He was brilliant (had eight patents) and often had questions they couldn't answer. When at seventeen, I announced to my parents that I wanted to go to Bible college to prepare for the pastorate, he was disappointed. He wanted me to become an engineer and work for his company. His alternative proposal was that I go to a nearby liberal arts university and delay deciding on a major for a year or two. If at that time, I still wanted to go to Bible college (which he doubted), then he would support my decision.

My experience at the university was what I expected. We listened to lectures, wrote papers, and took tests. However, midway through my first semester, I was convinced that I needed to transfer to Bible college. The theology I was being taught at the university was too liberal for me. In my naivety, I had expected someone would disciple me, even though I didn't exactly know what that meant. I assumed that at Bible college someone would train me for the ministry using similar methods as Jesus. Instead, we listened to lectures, wrote papers, and took tests.

Kings and Queens in the Kingdom of God

When I returned home after my first semester of Bible college, I told my dad, "I don't think they are doing it right." He laughed out loud, "You've been there one semester, and now you think you know more than they do?" Actually, I didn't know what I thought was wrong, but it just seemed insufficient. I didn't even know enough to frame the question. So, for the next three years, I listened to lectures, wrote papers, and took tests.

Seven years later, I had made it through both college and seminary, and still wondered why the academic institutions were preparing future pastors using the same methods as the secular universities. I assumed that pastors needed to be knowledgeable, but also something else. I knew enough that this "something else" wasn't being produced in me by listening to lectures, writing papers, and taking tests.

When researching for my thesis for my second master's, I finally developed a coherent question. I asked, "What have been the primary influences on the teaching methods used in Christian Education?" The answer I found was that there were several learning theories that have shaped Christian Education, all of them secular and humanistic. By humanistic, I mean that they believed ignorance is the problem and education is the sufficient solution to all the world's problems. But even I know that there are some things I know I should do, and I know how to do them, but I still don't do them.

If secular learning theories had moved Christian education away from the teaching methods of Jesus, then what would a Biblical learning theory look like? From a Christian perspective, ignorance is a problem, and education is necessary but not sufficient to solve our bigger problem: a lack of faith, or more specifically, sin. To explore this question, I decided I would have to go further than 'back to scratch,' I would have to go back to 'itch!'

Introduction

My next question was, "If education is supposed to prepare you for the future, what is Christian education supposed to prepare you to do?" Researching a Biblical answer to this question led me to Psalm 19:1-6 and Genesis 1:26-28, which ultimately led me to writing this book. Learning how to be a God-like ruler within the realm God has given you, all for His praise and glory, should be the goal of Christian education. *Becoming* a God-like ruler within the realm God has given you, all for His praise and glory, is another thing. That requires not only education but also transformation. How can we facilitate the transformation of our students, as well as provide Christian education to them? Well, I'm still working on that!

1

What is Wrong?

Recent events around the world have convinced everyone that something has gone wrong. Of course, there is no consensus on what is the "thing" that is so terribly wrong. Fingers are pointed in every direction, claiming some group, idea, or system has robbed us of the future we hoped for and believe we deserve. Solutions have ranged from "burn it all down" to "make it great again." Albert Einstein said, "We cannot solve our problems with the same thinking we used to create them."[1] I take this statement to mean that our problems are caused by faulty assumptions that are so embedded in our thinking that we are unaware that they are assumptions. At some point, to solve our biggest problems, we will need to dig down below what we have presumed to be bedrock truth, and search for long-forgotten questions and their answers underneath the bedrock. We need to ask ourselves about our own bedrock truths, our own personal assumptions.

---

1 Accessed on 10/3/20 from: https://www.brainyquote.com/authors/albert-einstein-quotes

Undiscovered Questions

Patrick hit the snooze button for the third time. He rolled over and saw his wife was already up and probably fixing breakfast for the kids. Their two incomes kept their credit card debt to a dull roar. He loved his kids even though the oldest was starting to get snarky. Mary seemed to be happy or at least satisfied with their marriage. It suddenly dawned on him that with the house, kids, and the dog, they had achieved the American dream in a very modest way.

He still wasn't ready to face another day at work, if that's what you want to call it. Patrick's job had long since become predictable - the same old stresses day after day. There were few challenges and fewer rewards. Patrick was a Christian but has never considered whether his beliefs have anything to do with being an accountant. His job paid the bills, and most of the people there were friendly enough, but somehow, he had presumed that his career would be more fulfilling. Instead, he felt empty.

Susan hung her jacket in the closet, and headed for the TV room to crash for the evening. She and Allen had just come home from celebrating their son's wedding. As happy as Susan was that her son had just "married up" to a wonderful girl, a gnawing feeling was rising in her chest that her future was suddenly a fog. Being a mom was the most rewarding thing she had done. But what now?

Allen and Susan's marriage had become comfortable. Allen's salary and her online business provided more than they needed. They tithed through their local church and even gave monthly to a missionary that had gone out from their church. Still, it seemed their Christian life was relegated mostly to attending and giving. Now that her son, Ryan, was out of the house and her online business was up and running,

What is Wrong?

she should have more time for something. She wished she could have more impact on eternal things. But how?

Hank returned to his church office. The service went well, and their numbers were up. He and Jill had planned their 40th wedding celebration and looked forward to seeing their kids and grandkids again. He hoped that getting away to the mountain resort they had planned would make up for the seventy-hour weeks that had become the norm. Committee meetings, hospital visits, volunteer recruitment, community events, attending the local high school games to support the youth, and their small group for young married couples has left Hank exhausted.

Hank reflected on the past month. As always, life was busy around the church. They had programs to meet a variety of needs and for the children and youth. Every new program meant more task forces, more budget lines, more recruitment of volunteers, and more committee meetings. He recalled when Jesus said, that He came that we might have life and life to the full. Somehow, he wasn't sure that all this busyness was what Jesus meant by "life to the full." His heart ached for this "fullness," but he was unsure what it would look like.

Bedrock Questions

One of my favorite quotes comes from Sir Francis Bacon. He wrote, "The significant question is the half of knowledge." In other words, you won't find the answer until you ask the right question. Patrick, Susan, and Hank were all beginning to ask significant questions: What does Christianity have to do with my career? How can we have an impact for eternity? What does it mean to live in God's fullness?

On the way to church, my four-year-old son asked from the back seat, "Dad, what's wrong?" Startled out of my preoccupied thoughts, I responded, "Nothing's wrong, Jon. Why do you ask?" He asked again,

"Dad, what's wrong?" Again, I tried to reassure him that everything was okay. Frustrated, he blurted out from behind me, "No, Dad, what's wrong? You need to teach me!"

I have often wished I could have gone back to that teachable moment and give a better answer to his question. At the time, I didn't realize that this young child was asking one of the most significant questions anyone could ask. Some questions just ask for facts. (i.e., What is your birthdate?) Some questions ask for opinions or beliefs. (i.e., What do you think the stock market will do this year?) But some questions ask for explanations for why the world is as it is and what it all means. These are what I call "bedrock questions." They ask about the meaning and purpose of it all. Your answers to bedrock questions ultimately reveal your assumptions about what is real and how the world works. The problem is that most people don't think deeply about how to answer them; they go on about their lives, assuming the answers they've been told but not considering the consequences of believing those answers. Depending on who you ask, these questions include, "Who am I?" "Where am I?" "Where did I come from?" "What makes something right or wrong?" "How do we solve what's wrong?" and "What happens when we die?".

In this book, I intend to explore possible answers to some of these questions in a way that will hopefully help answer Patrick's, Susan's, and Hank's questions. However, I believe that the best answers to these questions are found "below," whatever is commonly assumed to be the bedrock of what everybody "knows" to be true. When something isn't working, sometimes you have to "go back to scratch." However, to answer bedrock questions, we may need to "go back to itch."

For instance, to discover who we are, or at least who God intended us to be, we need to explore who we were before the fall of Adam. Only then can we begin to understand who we are becoming through

What is Wrong?

God's gracious restoration process. Let's start by looking at some common symptoms experienced by those not fulfilling God's initial plan. A typical symptom of living in a broken world is having a vague sense of emptiness. Somehow we sense that no matter how hard we try, we often feel empty and unfulfilled.

Empty People

Dr. J.P. Moreland described seven characteristics of an empty self.[2] When I read his list, my first thought was, (gulp), "I'm busted!" I thought I had a very fulfilling life. I was fully engaged in my ideal job (teaching at a Christian college), had a loving family and plenty of friends. I was planting a house church with some of my students, mentoring other students, was an elder in my local church, financially stable, enjoying hobbies like golf and woodworking, and trying to find time to write a book (the one you are reading). It is not like I identified with all of the things on the list, but one or two of the seven hit me pretty hard. I realized I was more busy than fulfilled.

One word of caution: These seven characteristics are just examples of how some people respond to the feeling of emptiness. Moreland's point is that we tend to respond to a sense of emptiness without realizing what feeling we are responding to. And, of course, each of us responds to our feelings a little differently. See if any of the following are familiar to you.

1. Empty people do not want to depend on anyone for help

Emptiness causes a feeling of incompleteness. Empty people sense that something is missing, but they don't know what. Feeling that some-

---

[2] J.P. Moreland, Love Your God with All Your Mind, "The Role of Reason in the Life of the Soul," (Colorado Springs: NavPress, 2012).

thing is missing, in turn, causes insecurity and the fear that something is wrong with them. Insecure people tend to hide what they perceive as weakness. The result is that they make self-sufficiency and independence from others a high personal value. There is nothing wrong with being self-sufficient in many areas of our lives, but if it keeps us from seeking help when we need it, an independent spirit can keep us from experiencing fulness.

Hank, the busy pastor, has fallen into this trap. Out of a lack of faith that God can use others to lead essential ministries, Hank assumes that he has to lead almost every ministry of the church. To set boundaries on how many ministries he can personally lead would be an acknowledgment of his own limits. He is too insecure about delegating leadership to others and unwilling to admit that the church had launched ministries on the pastor's back before God provided the leaders he had in mind. Pastor Hank could have experienced great fulfillment by seeing God affirm the need for these new ministries by providing the needed leaders and then supporting and mentoring those leaders to bear much fruit.

2. Empty people insist on instant gratification, comfort, and soothing

Emptiness causes angst or hunger for something more. Empty people self-medicate the pain in many different ways. For some, it is comfort food. Other empty people self-medicate with pornography, drugs, or gambling. Or with not-so-guilty pleasures such as hobbies, DIY projects, sports, or anything that gives them an adrenaline rush mixed with dopamine and serotonin, the neurotransmitters associated with pleasure and a sense of well-being. In essence, empty people live for instant pleasure and are willing to take shortcuts to get immediate relief from having to face their emptiness.

What is Wrong?

Susan and Allen's passive church attendance and giving out of their financial abundance could be an example of this type of emptiness. Taking in the worship music and sermon before dropping a sizable check in the offering is a "churchy" way to get a quick buzz of self-righteousness. However, the distance they keep from personal involvement in the ministry is a missed opportunity to experience lasting fulfillment. They have spiritual gifts that God wants to use, but most effective ministries are "messy." Broken people often have "hard to heal" problems that require a lot of love and patience. It is so much easier to attend twice a month and write a check.

3. Empty people believe everything is about them

Emptiness causes an inward focus. That is where the pain is coming from and where they focus their attention. Empty people assume that though the pain resides inside them, the source of their pain must be from outside them. Therefore, they are quick to find fault with everything and everyone around them. They have this pervasive hope of finding something or someone who can be used to their benefit. The constant search for something or someone to fill their emptiness keeps their focus on the question, "What can you do for me?"

Patrick, the bored accountant, feels that his emptiness is caused by his job or at least the company he works for. From his perspective, the problem is his unfulfilling job. This is typical of Gen Y employees, but also many in other generations. Paul Harvey, a University of New Hampshire professor and Gen Y expert, has researched this. He found that Gen Y has "unrealistic expectations and a strong resistance toward accepting negative feedback" and "an inflated view of oneself." He says that "a great source of frustration for people with a strong sense of entitlement is unmet expectations. They often feel entitled to a level of respect and rewards that aren't in line with their actual ability and effort levels, and so they might not get the level of respect and rewards they are expecting."[3] Empty people are self-centered and expect fulfillment will come to them naturally, and when it doesn't, the problem is someone else's fault.

4. Empty people are passive – want to be amused

The ability to focus your attention on something is a limited resource. Investing your time, energy, and resources on things that leave you feeling empty quickly burns up that limited resource. Experiencing fulfillment replenishes your ability to focus your attention. It enables you to think, plan, and problem-solve. Empty people frequently feel burnt out and don't have the strength to think about the source of their emptiness. That is why they want to be entertained or amused. "To muse" means "to think." When you put the negative prefix "a" in front of the word, it becomes "amuse" or "to not think." I think we all have reached a state of exhaustion where we "just don't want to think about it now" and then turn to a mindless activity like TV or video games. That is when we need to do something fulfilling, like connecting with loved ones or simply getting some sleep.

Pastor Hank is definitely experiencing burnout. He believes that a vacation will solve the problem of 70 hour work weeks. It may give him some relief... until Monday morning when he returns to the office to find his absence has left him buried again.

---

[3] Tim Urban, Why Generation Y Yuppies are Unhappy, Accessed on 6/16/21 from: https://waitbutwhy.com/2013/09/why-generation-y-yuppies-are-unhappy.html

5. Empty people only believe things that can be experienced through the senses

Moreland explains that there are two types of cultures, sensate and ideational.[4] In sensate cultures, people believe that the only things that are real are the things we can see, hear, smell, taste, or touch. In ideational cultures, people accept the reality of immaterial reality, including God, the soul, supernatural beings, and things like propositions, values, and purposes. Once people reject the possibility of having a greater purpose outside themselves, they eventually lose any concept of fulfillment except the pleasures experienced through the senses. As a result, they lose hope that their angst will ever go away. Some, then, turn to violence and rage to both fill their senses and express their frustration.

The loss that Susan is experiencing is a loss of purpose. Without her belief in God, Susan might seek to fill her emptiness through spending money, become a workaholic, or just several half-gallons of ice cream. This is a critical time for her to seek God's direction for her future. Experiencing significant loss will sometimes spin even Christians into depression. The tendency then is to counter the physical effects of depression with activities that release dopamine and serotonin. The problem is that reaching the bottom of the ice cream carton still leaves you feeling empty.

6. Empty people are more concerned with how others perceive them than their actual moral character

Because empty people realize they are hollow, they find ways to put on a positive front. Almost anyone can create a glowing online persona. It is so much easier to appear impressive than to be someone who others would respect and honor. Their goal is not self-improvement as much

---

[4] J.P. Moreland, Love Your God with All Your Mind, "The Role of Reason in the Life of the Soul," (Colorado Springs: NavPress, 2012), p. 106.

as gaining the power associated with being influential. For them, it is more about "lookin' good" than character development.

Patrick, the accountant, had pursued the "American Dream." Why? Because that is what prosperous and respectable people do. Susan had made sure her church attendance was noted and appreciated because of her giving. Hank hoped that a successful ministry could hide any damage to his marriage and family. All three found it easier to impress others than to seek actual fulfillment. However, seeking true fulfillment is not necessarily a selfish act. It is the result of bringing glory to God by doing what God designed us to do. The difference is whether we do things for the purpose of fulfillment, or we find fulfilment as a result of doing what God designed us to do.

7. Empty people stay busy to avoid meaningful relationships and awareness of their emptiness

Finally, all of the above causes empty people to find comfort in a hectic life. This sounds counter intuitive. Who would want a hurried and over busy life? It seems many people do because they repeatedly make choices that produce that kind of life. Of course, they then proceed to complain about it! Their hectic schedule takes their attention away from their pain while at the same time giving them an excuse for not wanting to engage in meaningful relationships, which could dangerously expose their emptiness to others.

Writing to believers, Apostle Peter reminded them that they "were redeemed from the empty way of life handed down to you from your ancestors… with the precious blood of Christ." Because followers of Christ don't carry the burden of depending solely on ourselves but instead can "cast all our cares upon him," there is no need for us to experience emptiness. Because as Children of God, we receive comfort from the Holy Spirit in the middle of our trials, there is no need for us to experience emptiness. As members of the Kingdom who live to glorify God rather than ourselves, there is no need for us to experience emptiness. Because we, who are called out of the darkness and into the light have hope in the resurrection, there is no need for us to experience emptiness. Because we freely acknowledge that we are a work in progress, being transformed in our inner being, and yet enjoy meaningful relationships by speaking the truth in love to each other, there is no need for us to experience emptiness.

And yet, sometimes we do. I believe that is because the church has lost clarity on how we were designed to fulfill God's purpose for the human race. Since Aquinas, the church has taught us that there is sacred work and secular work. Secular work is what we do to provide materially for ourselves, but sacred work is "ministry." This dogma not only produced the division between clergy and the laity, but also led believers to compartmentalize their lives into the spiritual things that Jesus rules and the material things which we rule. So how do we fill our emptiness? That's what this book will teach you.

An Incomplete Gospel

Patrick laid in bed for five more minutes, wondering about what God expected of him today. As he thought through the rest of his day, he remembered that he had a monthly P & L report due by the end of the day, a meeting with the shipping supervisor at 11:00, and several emails needing his response. Where was God in all of that? Why is there so much of my 9 to 5 life that never gets covered in the preacher's sermons?

Susan and Allen were eating breakfast the next day. Susan was still hurting from walking past their son's empty room. She has been replaced by a beautiful and talented bride. Susan longed to have a new purpose in life but certainly wasn't ready to go to Africa as a missionary. She found a lot of fulfillment in her blossoming company. Why couldn't God use her through her business?

Hank looked at his overflowing in-basket. As pastor of the church, there were bills to read and pass onto the trustees, budgets to prepare for next year, monthly reports to the elders, payroll hours of the staff to approve, emails to respond to, and cards to sign congratulating the graduating seniors. Besides all the paperwork, Hank needed to research the ministries that other churches were doing, like the one they felt God was calling them to next. Hank knew all this "stuff" would keep him in the office for the rest of the day. He leaned back in his chair and asked himself, "Is this ministry? Is this what God had in mind when he called me to be a pastor?"

Patrick, Susan, and maybe even Hank might be suffering from an incomplete gospel. The gospel they have believed is the good news that by faith and through God's glorious grace, Jesus Christ, through His substitutionary atonement for our sins, has provided a way for them to reunite with God. The focus of that gospel is on restoring the relationship between God and us so that God can transform us into the image of Christ. I believe in that gospel, but I also think that this gospel, as stated above, addresses only part of what God is doing in our restoration.

This limited gospel is a significant cause of an attitude of Sunday only consumerism in many believers today. They presume that Jesus came to restore only our souls or spirits. Sunday only consumers spend most Sunday mornings maintaining their spiritual life. Since their spiritual life is only part of their life, it only requires part of their time (Sunday mornings) to maintain it. Of course, you have to keep things in balance. For instance, there is a time for work or school, a time for

What is Wrong?

play, and a time for worship– or so this attitude assumes. Accordingly, worship is what you do in church, not on the job or around the house.

Like any good consumer, they seek to find the best value for their time and money. That leads them to attend a church only as long as they feel like they are getting their needs met. Are the services uplifting? Are the sermons helpful? Are there quality programs to meet their particular needs?

To select our primary grocery store, we would ask ourselves similar questions. Is the selection enough for what you want? Do I enjoy the people who work there? Is it in a convenient location? What are the specials this week? These are appropriate questions for selecting a grocery store, but when used to determine where to go to church, they reveal a consumer-oriented mindset.

I have always hated to be labeled as a consumer. It is not that I don't consume products and services from our economy, but it makes me feel like a parasite. It doesn't acknowledge what I contribute to society. Many of us were taught from childhood that we are to always give more value than we receive, to leave the world a better place than we found it. We all want to think that we are more producers than consumers.

Ideas have consequences. Suppose believers typically see themselves as consumers of spiritual ministries. In that case, churches will market themselves to spiritual consumers to compete for their dollars and derrieres in the pews. When the purpose of a church is to attract spiritual consumers, the gospel they preach shrinks to addressing only the message that they can spoon feed to passive attendees. That is when bodies, buildings, and budgets become the measure of success rather than changed lives.

I heard a saying at a church multiplication seminar that I think very simply illustrates how the church got where it is today:

> The church started in Jerusalem as a community
> It moved to Greece and became a philosophy
> It moved to Rome and became a system
> It moved to Europe and became an art form
> It moved to America and became a business
> It is time for the church to return to being a community.

If the church returned to being a community, then its members would live life together. Not necessarily communally, sharing money and housing, but rather being involved with each other's whole lives, not just their spiritual life. They would be helping each other through the stages of life, praying for each other, mourning each other's losses, and celebrating each other's good times.

However, moving the church from being a business of providing services for spiritual consumers to being an interactive community will require a significant change. The gospel will need to be restored to encompass all of our life and not just our spiritual life. It will need to address why relationships are so important, why we work, and how we can glorify God through everything we do.

Synthetic Happiness

There comes the point in my Introduction to Psychology class in which I ask my students, "How many of you have become all that you've ever wanted to be?" With my hand in the air, I tell them, "Raise your hands if you think you have." The deer-in-the-headlights stares reveal their confusion about even being asked the question. Then I lower my hand and confess that I, too, am still a work in progress. The humanistic perspective in psychology is based on the observation people often do what they do because they are trying to become someone they are not yet. We have an innate drive to become something or someone that still eludes us.

What is Wrong?

What do you want? Most of my college students don't know how to answer that question. I can make it easier for them by putting the question in context. What do you want for lunch today? What do you want from this class? Most only want an A and never mention what they want to learn. However, if the context gets too large, for instance, "What do you want in a career? What do you want in a marriage? What are your financial goals?" Many, if not most of them, have no clue what they want. They haven't thought much about the bigger questions.

There are a couple of reasons why we don't dwell on our wants. First, somehow we absorb the idea that wanting is selfish. An unfortunate translation of Psalm 23:1, "The Lord is my Shepherd, I shall not want," makes it sound as though we shouldn't have "wants." Secondly, being specific about what you want is a scary commitment. What if you get what you said you wanted but are still not fulfilled?

What exactly is "fulfillment?" Vocabulary.com defines fulfillment as "a feeling of happiness and satisfaction."[5] Many people assume that fulfillment is a feeling– the emotion of being "happy." Further, we often assume that happiness is the result of getting what you want. The pursuit of happiness is one of our "inalienable rights" mentioned in the Declaration of Independence. Thomas Jefferson never questioned that people would want to pursue happiness.

So, how do you pursue happiness? What do you think will make you happy? How did you come to that conclusion? We all have seen people on social media or others around you who have what you want and seem to be happier than you are. The natural assumption is that it is the state of "not having" that makes us unhappy.

Harvard professor, Dan Gilbert, theorized that happiness is so important to us that if we don't get what we want, we will still find a

---

[5] Vocabulary.com. Accessed 6/26/19 from: https://www.vocabulary.com/dictionary/fulfillment

way to believe we are happy regardless of our situation.[6] He calls it "synthetic happiness." His research indicates little difference between the self-reported level of happiness of those who have had devastating losses (they were asked after they have had a chance to adjust to their new circumstances) and people who have had wonderful lives. During the period of adjustment, the people who had suffered huge financial, political, or personal losses were able to re-evaluate their perspective and find enough positives to be happy despite their losses. If we can (and typically do) synthetically create our happiness regardless of our circumstances, then happiness becomes a meaningless self-provided wash of dopamine and serotonin through the brain. According to Gilbert's research, happiness depends solely on your ability to rationalize the goodness of your circumstances. That's not a bad thing, but it shows the difference between happiness and fulfillment.

One strategy to identify the path to fulfillment is to give examples of apparently happy people who already have what we think we want. The media loves to dangle "picture perfect lives" before our eyes, and yet these stories often fuel our unhappiness, reminding us of what we do not have. Of course on the other side, we could also find examples of unhappy people who already have all the things we want. The rich and famous also struggle with marriage problems, depression, and addiction. These stories ring true to us because they make these people seem more real to us, but they leave us feeling empty. If they have what we want but are unhappy, why should we even try? Likewise, as in Dan Gilbert's book, there are instances of people who have what we don't want but report that they are happy anyway. Clearly, getting what you want does not correlate with being happy. Further, happiness does not appear to be the same thing as being fulfilled. The worldly view is that fulfillment is a feeling of happiness combined with satisfaction. But,

---

6 Dan Gilbert, Stumbling on Happiness, (New York: Vintage Books, 2006).

What is Wrong?

is a particular feeling all we want? Or are we looking for an objective evaluation of whether we have accomplished what we were designed to do.

Daniel Gilbert made another observation about the relationship of value judgments and happiness,

> "We cannot say that something is good unless we can say what it is good for, and if we examine all the many objects and experiences that our species calls good and ask what they are good for, the answer is clear: By and large, they are good for making us feel happy."[7]

If we as Christians define "good" as anything that makes us happy, then we are no different from the world whom Gilbert accurately described. However, as Peter wrote, we have been "redeemed from the empty way of life handed down to you from your ancestors." We have a greater purpose than just making ourselves happy.

An underlying principle of this book is that many people waste time, money, health, and relationships in unsuccessful pursuits of fulfillment. Jesus said, "The thief comes only to steal and kill and destroy; I have come that they may have life, and have it to the full."[8] Satan wants to rob us of meaning, purpose, and value. Unfortunately, many people believe his lies and come to the end of their lives, wondering if there is any meaning, purpose, and value to life.

On the flip side, another underlying principle of this book is that there is a way to pursue fulfillment as God intended. As I said above, seeking true fulfillment is not a selfish act. It is the result of bringing glory to God by doing what God designed us to do. Let's be clear. I'm not the one guaranteeing your fulfillment, but my purpose in writing

---

[7] Dan Gilbert, Stumbling on Happiness, (New York: Vintage Books, 2006), 78.
[8] John 10:10 (NIV)

this book is to help you find a path where, by faith and following, God will fill you as much as you are willing to receive. True fulfillment, rather than synthetic happiness, is possible.

This is not to say we can't be both fulfilled and happy, but rather that they are two separate things. God wants something better for you. He wants you to experience a feeling deeper than happiness called joy. Joy fills us with more than just being happy.

Joy is a fruit of the Spirit (Galatians 5:22). In other words, as we allow the Spirit to form Christ in us, we will experience greater and greater joy. Joy and happiness are significantly different. Happiness is a pleasurable feeling. However, we can experience joy in spite of unpleasant circumstances. The testimonies of this are endless. Typically, Christians filled with joy despite painful circumstances, explain that they are joyful because a greater good (that God would be glorified) will come from their circumstances. Apostle Peter noted this was true of the early Christians:

> In all this you greatly rejoice, though now for a little while you may have had to suffer grief in all kinds of trials. These have come so that the proven genuineness of your faith—of greater worth than gold, which perishes even though refined by fire—may result in praise, glory and honor when Jesus Christ is revealed. (1 Peter 1:6-9)

Joy is more like a sense of well-being based on a confidence that you are accomplishing your purpose of glorifying God, even though it may be in the context of painful circumstances.

A third underlying principle of this book is that just as form follows function, so also fulfillment follows effective functioning. Let me explain. A hammer is shaped differently than a paintbrush. Trying to pound in a nail with a paintbrush will not work very well. The bristles won't have much of an impact on the nail. The form of a hammer is

What is Wrong?

designed to fulfill its function. Likewise, we have been designed with a function in mind. In fact, all of creation has been formed to fulfill one ultimate function. Each part of creation, every galaxy, star, planet, species, and individual, is uniquely shaped to play its unique part in fulfilling the ultimate function of glorifying God. Understanding and effectively playing your specific role in humanity's designed function is the key to experiencing true fulfillment.

Kings and Queens in the Kingdom of God

Discussion Questions

1. Of the seven characteristics of empty people, which do you think best describes you?
   - Empty people do not want to depend on anyone for help
   - Empty people insist on instant gratification, comfort, and soothing
   - Empty people believe everything is about them
   - Empty people are passive– want to be amused
   - Empty people only believe things that can be experienced through the senses
   - Empty people are more concerned with how others perceive them than their actual moral character
   - Empty people stay busy to avoid meaningful relationships and awareness of their emptiness

What is Wrong?

2. What are some of the tasks you do every week that seem unrelated to your faith?

3. How do you pursue happiness?

4. What talent, gift, or experience has God given you to be part of your "story" for His glory?

2

Becoming Kings and Queens

What's your fantasy? Have you ever pondered, "If I were king or queen for a day, I would…"? We start having fantasies when we are children, and they usually are built on the theme that everyone else has to do what we want them to do. That fantasy might be all about getting your personal desires fulfilled. However, if your fantasy becomes making the world right again, it will probably focus on everyone believing what you want them to believe. In other words, we fantasize about everyone seeing the world and how it is supposed to work the same way we see it.

Part of the reason our society is so polarized is that we fundamentally disagree on the answers to these bedrock questions. Consider some of the typical beliefs expressed by secularists (people who believe God does not exist, or at least he is irrelevant). For instance, they tend to accept the "Big Bang" as an explanation of the origin of our universe. Secularists also assume that the variety of species that exist today (including humans) have evolved by chance over billions of years. Finally, many secularists believe that society's problems (e.g., poverty, crime, and war) are caused by the structure of that society and not necessarily by the character of the individuals who make up that society. Therefore, they seek solutions to a society's problems by challenging the society's traditional values and institutions.

There are logical consequences of these beliefs. First, if eight billion other people on this planet and I have resulted from the big bang and evolution by chance, there is no objective meaning to the universe. The only meaning left is what something means to me and others who agree with me. Additionally, there is no design to tell us how things are supposed to be, they just are. If there is no ultimate design of the universe, there is no ultimate purpose. The only purpose left is what I, or once again the people who agree with me, choose as a purpose. As a result, there is no absolute right or wrong. Right is then determined by the purpose they have chosen for themselves. If something is "right," it is because it aligns with their chosen purpose. If something is "wrong," it is because it is contrary to that purpose. But, whose purpose? Do I get to choose? Does the government?

Finally, if God is absent from the picture and society has been full of disease, poverty, crime, and war for as long as we know, then we are our only hope for the future. To sustain this hope, we would have to believe that we as individuals have what it takes to solve society's problems. In other words, the patient must become the doctor. We would have to believe that we could raise ourselves by our bootstraps to a higher plane of existence. This would require me to believe that people (most importantly, me) are essentially good, and the problem is somehow outside of me. The problem with that is… I know better.

There are two reasons secularists might not want to think about the consequences of their beliefs. First, it could make them feel insignificant, being only one person among billions of people on one planet in a solar system among billions of other solar systems in just one galaxy among billions of others. Second, it could make them feel hopeless. I can imagine them thinking, "If we've always had these problems, why do we believe we could ever solve them? And, if the universe is eventually going to grow cold and die, what is the use of trying?" These thoughts typically lead secularists to fantasize about two possible solutions:

1. I will be able to carve out my own little "kingdom" protected from society's problems (e.g., living in a gated community and having unending wealth), or
2. Some new technological, political, or economic systems will eventually eliminate disease, crime, poverty, and war.

A Christian Answer

We don't have to be insignificant and hopeless or retreat into a fantasy world. Jesus came preaching the good news about a coming kingdom that will solve all of these problems (Matthew 4:23). As we were taught, we pray, "Thy Kingdom come, Thy will be done." I confess that for most of my Christian life, when I prayed that prayer, my focus was on either asking Jesus to come back soon to set up his kingdom or to get out of this crazy world and into his kingdom.

Eventually, I became aware that the Kingdom of God is already here, and I am part of it. The Kingdom of God is not someplace for me to escape to. It is the presence of Jesus with me as I go through this life. John Ortberg notes that our race has always wanted to know, "What's our story?" "Who is our God?" "Why are we here?"[9] So, speaking only for myself as a follower of Jesus, I would answer these questions differently than a secularist:

I am formed in God's image as part of God's amazing creation that was designed in both its unimaginable vastness and in mi-

---

9 John Ortberg (2018). Eternity is Now in Session. Carol Stream, IL: Tyndale House Publishers. p. 132.

croscopic detail to display the glory of God. This creation was broken by Adam's sin but is being redeemed by Jesus Christ to create a new heaven and earth through the Kingdom of God. I am a child of God by adoption through the work of the Holy Spirit and a subject to Christ, the King of Kings, with whom I will reign forever and ever.

My answer assumes that God is relevant to my everyday life as well as my future. It reveals I have meaning and purpose because I was designed to glorify God, along with the rest of creation. However, just as each species has its unique way of glorifying God, I am uniquely designed to glorify God as a God-like ruler (Genesis 1:26-28). However, as part of a broken world, I too am broken and need redemption, but I place my hope in God, my King, and my Redeemer. Finally, this answer reveals my significance (as a subject of the King) and my hope for the future: reigning with Christ forever.

But what about my hope for today and the rest of this week? How do I merge the stories of the Bible with being an accountant, a farmer, an electrician, or a teacher? What does the Kingdom of God have to do with Mondays through Saturdays? What hope do I have that what I do most of the week really matters and can glorify God? And finally, what exactly is the Kingdom of God?

What is the Kingdom of God?

Some theologians say the Kingdom of God is only spiritual, something we experience "inside." Others say it is now the invisible true church or the social gospel righting all the wrongs in this world. Still, others say that the Kingdom of God will come when Jesus returns.[10] George Eldon Ladd in his classic book, The Gospel of the Kingdom,

---

10 Nicholas Perrin (2019). The Kingdom of God, a Biblical theology. Grand Rapids, MI: Zondervan. pp. 23-24.

claimed the Bible affirms that the Kingdom of God is part of all of these. Romans 14:7 says, "For the kingdom of God is not a matter of eating and drinking, but of righteousness, peace and joy in the Holy Spirit." This passage explains that the Kingdom of God is experienced spiritually. In the letter to the church in Colossae, Paul wrote, "For he has rescued us from the dominion of darkness and brought us into the kingdom of the Son he loves" (Colossians 1:13). This makes it clear that those who are in the church, seeking to follow Christ, are also in the kingdom. James also points out that religion that is acceptable to God, takes care of those in need, such as orphans and widows (James 1:27). So, the subjects of the Kingdom of God are called to help fill needs in our society. And finally, Peter encourages us about a future time when we will enter into the kingdom, "For if you do these things, you will never stumble, and you will receive a rich welcome into the eternal kingdom of our Lord and Savior Jesus Christ (1 Peter 1:10-11).[11] So, the Kingdom of God is both present and yet to come. It is also spiritual and yet meets the physical needs in our society.

John Ortberg notes that everyone has a kingdom. Your kingdom is that little sphere in which what you say goes. It is the range of your effective will. He then defines the Kingdom of God as the range of God's effective will, wherever God's will is done[12]. This definition is essentially correct, but there is so much more to it. It would be like defining a mother simply as a person who birthed a baby.[13]

---

11 George Eldon Ladd (1959). The Gospel of the Kingdom, Scriptural studies in the Kingdom of God. Grand Rapids, MI: Eerdmans Publishing Co. pp. 16-18.
12 John Ortberg (2018). Eternity is Now in Session. Carol Stream, IL: Tyndale House Publishers. pp. 20-21.
13 O.Palmer Robertson (1980). The Christ of the Covenants. Phillipsburg, N.J.: Presbyterian and Reformed Publishing Co., p.3.

N.T. Wright proposed that the Kingdom of God began with the exodus. It was when the one true God "made himself known in power, defeating the powers of evil, and rescuing his people. It speaks of what, in later scriptures, came to be called the Kingdom of God." Wright acknowledged that God was already the "rightful ruler of the world," but at this point in history, God became king in a whole new way to "reclaim his kingdom after the power of evil had usurped it[14]. I find this argument compelling because God began at the exodus to collect a people to know and follow him. He was physically intervening on their behalf and setting up a priestly system by which he could rule these people as their king. However, there is also a compelling argument that the Kingdom of God began at creation.

Did the Kingdom of God begin at Creation?

Just as we might consider it hard to understand a kingdom with no king, Nicholas Perrin suggested that the ancients would consider "the idea of a kingdom without a covenant to be as equally absurd."[15] A kingdom can only be established through a mutually beneficial covenant between the king and his subjects. The king seeks the service of loyal subjects, and his subjects seek the leadership of the king to protect them from enemies and to establish justice within the kingdom. This begs the question, "When was the first covenant between God and humans?" One answer could be the Noahic covenant (Genesis 9:9) because this is the first time that the word "covenant" (mekim) was used in the Old Testament. However, there is a compelling argument that the act of creation established a covenantal relationship between God and all of creation.

---

14 N.T. Wright (2015). Simply Good News, Why the gospel is news and what makes it good. New York: HarperCollins. p. 36.
15 Nicholas Perrin (2019). The Kingdom of God, a Biblical theology. Grand Rapids, MI: Zondervan. p. 58.

Palmer Robertson defines a covenant as "a bond in blood sovereignly administered."[16] By "a bond in blood," he means a bond of life and death which expresses the ultimate nature of the commitment. By "sovereignly administered," he notes that there is no bartering or negotiation in the divine covenants. The Lord sovereignly dictates the terms of the covenant. Jonathan Lunde explained that there are two types of covenants: "grant covenants," which are unconditional, and "conditional covenants." In a grant covenant, the grantor is totally responsible for carrying out the terms of the covenant and does not require the obedience of the recipient of the covenant. In a conditional covenant, both parties are responsible, and disobedience to the covenant terms must result in the death of the disobedient party.[17]

Was Creation a Covenant?

Let's then observe the creation story to determine if it meets the criteria of either type of covenant. First, God sovereignly ruled over His creation. He did not set up a democracy, giving the various parts of creation, such as the fish, the birds, or the land animals, a vote to determine who would rule all of the creation next. Therefore, if the process of creation was a covenant, it was sovereignly administered. Since God created the universe, he had the right to do with it whatever he wanted (Romans 9:20-21).

Second, there were conditions placed upon the creatures He made. He blessed and commanded the fish and the birds, "Be fruitful and increase in number and fill the water in the seas, and let the birds increase on the earth" (Genesis 1:22). But to humans, He gave more

---

16 O. Palmer Robertson (1980). *The Christ of the Covenants*. Phillipsburg, N.J.: Presbyterian and Reformed Publishing Co., p. 4.
17 Jonathan Lunde (2010). *Following Jesus, the Servant King*. Grand Rapids, MI: Zondervan. p. 39-40.

Kings and Queens in the Kingdom of God

specific conditions they were designed and commanded to fulfill. Genesis 1:26-28 reads,

> Then God said, "Let us make mankind in our image, in our likeness, so that they may rule over the fish in the sea and the birds in the sky, over the livestock and all the wild animals, and over all the creatures that move along the ground."
> So God created mankind in his own image,
> in the image of God he created them;
> male and female he created them.
> God blessed them and said to them, "Be fruitful and increase in number; fill the earth and subdue it. Rule over the in the sea and the birds in the sky and over every living creature that moves on the ground."

Further conditions placed upon Adam are revealed in Genesis 2:15-17:

> The Lord God took the man and put him in the Garden of Eden to work it and take care of it. And the Lord God commanded the man, "You are free to eat from any tree in the garden; but you must not eat from the tree of the knowledge of good and evil, for when you eat from it you will certainly die."

The death penalty God prescribed for eating the fruit of the tree of good and evil certainly made this a "bond of blood sovereignly administered," specifically a conditional covenant. Perrin agrees that creation is a covenant and comments, "If the Noahic covenant may be seen as a kind of rider of the covenant of creation, then we might surmise that all of the covenants, including the Abrahamic covenant, are in fact successive steps in unfolding God's creational purposes."[18]

---

18 Nicholas Perrin (2019). The Kingdom of God, a Biblical theology. Grand Rapids, MI: Zondervan. p. 58.

Becoming Kings and Queens

In the creation covenant, God grants three things to Adam's race. First, God granted to humans that they would bear the image and likeness of God. Through this likeness, humans were made priests unto God, able to communicate with Him. Second, God granted humans to be kings and queens with a realm to rule. They were to "rule over the fish in the sea and the birds in the sky, over the livestock and all the wild animals, and overall the creatures that move along the ground" (Gen 1: 26). Third, for their food, he granted "every seed-bearing plant on the face of the whole earth and every tree that has fruit with seed in it" (Gen 1:29), and more specifically, the fruit of every tree in the garden, except the fruit from the tree of the knowledge of good and evil (Gen 2:17).

Therefore, I believe there is a compelling argument that the Kingdom God began with creation as a conditional covenant. God designed humans to represent Him on earth as kings and queens within the Kingdom of God, each with our own realm but still subject to the King of Kings. We were also designed to be royal priests who communicate with God and represent God to the rest of creation. Being sons of God, we are to pass our authority and responsibility to future generations by inheritance. God commanded Adam and Eve to "be fruitful and increase in number; fill the earth and subdue it." However, instead of bringing life to the earth, the breaking of the Creation Covenant resulted in the introduction of both physical and spiritual death. The rest of this book explores the character of our fallen royalty, how we are specifically designed to glorify God by filling the earth and subduing it, and how God is restoring us to our rightful thrones. In other words, to rule as God rules.

Kings and Queens in the Kingdom of God

Discussion Questions

1. If you were king or queen for a day, what would you do? What problem would you try to solve?

2. What are some of the benefits you receive by belonging to the Kingdom of God?

3. If God intended us to rule over the "the fish in the sea and the birds in the sky, over the livestock and all the wild animals, and over all the creatures that move along the ground," when did ruling become ruling over other people?

4. What are some things that "fill the earth and subdue it" could involve? What do you think it probably does not mean?

3

What's Your Story?

At the end of chapter one, I mentioned that all of creation had been formed to fulfill one ultimate function. Each part of creation, every galaxy, star, planet, species, and individual is uniquely shaped to play its unique part in fulfilling one ultimate function. So, what is this "ultimate function" we all have been designed to fulfill?

In 1765, Jonathan Edwards published a book on "The End for Which God Created the World." In it, he wrote:

> "It appears that all that is ever spoken of in the Scripture as an ultimate end of God's works is included in that one phrase, the glory of God... In the creature's knowing, esteeming, loving, rejoicing in, and praising God, the glory of God is both exhibited and acknowledged; his fullness is received and returned."

John Piper commented on the above statement, "That is the heart of Jonathan Edwards and, I believe, of the Bible too ...And it is the essence of what is needed today to overcome the hollowing out of evangelical life and the collapsing of our private meditations into self-centered musings."[19] Edwards understood that our ultimate func-

---

19 Jonathan Edwards, "The End for Which God Created the World," 252,

tion is to tell the story of God's glory. Perhaps our journey toward restoration depends in part upon discovering how God has specifically designed you and me to tell part of the glory of God. Of course, it takes all of creation to tell this story.

Psalm 19:1-4 gives us a glimpse into this ultimate function of creation,

> The heavens declare the glory of God;
> the skies proclaim the work of his hands.
> Day after day they pour forth speech;
> night after night they reveal knowledge.
> They have no speech, they use no words;
> no sound is heard from them.
> Yet their voice goes out into all the earth,
> their words to the ends of the world.

There are clues in the original Hebrew of these verses that indicate more than is expressed in this translation. First, the word translated "declare" is in an intensive form meaning to give a full accounting rather than a cursory one.[20] Second, the word translated "proclaim" meant to place previously unknown information in the center of everyone's attention.[21] Finally, the word translated "pour" meant "an

---

in John Piper, God's Passion for His Glory, Living the Vision of Jonathan Edwards, (Wheaton, IL: Crossways Books, 1998), 92.

20 The Hebrew word, saphar, is in the Piel form in this verse which according to J. Weingreen, A Practical Grammar for Classical Hebrew, (Oxford: Clarendon Press), 100, indicates intensive action. R.D. Patterson in R. Laird Harris, Gleason Archer, and Bruce Waltke, eds., Theological Wordbook of the Old Testament (Chicago: Moody Press, 1980), 2:633, writes that saphar is used of "general mathematical activity and that in the Piel stem, the iterative concept, "recount," takes on the additional idea of "tell," "declare," "show forth." When considering the intensive action of the Piel, the implication is to give a full accounting rather than a cursory one.

21 The Hebrew word, nagah, according to Leanard Coppes in R. Laird Harris, Gleason Archer, and Bruce Waltke, eds., Theological Wordbook

uncontrollable or uncontrolled gushing forth," like a stream that has flooded beyond its banks.[22] A paraphrase of verses one and two could be,

> Through His creation, God is giving a full accounting, telling a full and long story about His glory by bringing new information to our attention, and is bubbling with excitement to have this story told.

God wants every part of creation, including you and me, to fulfill our role as royal priests by telling our part of the story of God's glory. I don't necessarily mean giving our testimony, although that could be the part some of us are to play. Rather, I mean that each of us has a unique part of the story to be told by how we interact with everything around us and respond to all that happens to us. Our thoughts and attitudes speak volumes about the extent that we glorify God as His image on earth.

As Psalm 19 reminds us, all of nature is telling the story of God's glory without using words. Every species, planet, star, and galaxy is a fingerprint of God. Their design and their symbiotic relationships reveal the glory of His wisdom and power. Archaeologists interpret human artifacts from ancient cultures to discover the beliefs and practices of those ancient people. In a sense, as we scientifically observe

---

of the Old Testament, (Chicago: Moody Press, 1980), 2:549-550, meant, "to place a matter high, conspicuous before a person... usually the "matter" was previously unknown or unknowable to the object... Divine glory (Ps19:1; 97:6) and righteousness (Ps 50:6) are made known and brought to prominence by the visible creation (cf. Rom 1:18ff.)."

22 The Hebrew word, nabah, according to Leanard Coppes in R. Laird Harris, Gleason Archer, and Bruce Waltke, eds., Theological Wordbook of the Old Testament, (Chicago: Moody Press, 1980), 2: 548 means "an uncontrollable or uncontrolled gushing forth as, e.g. the swollen waters of a wadi. In Ps 19:2, nabah images the "uninterrupted line of transmission" and "inexhaustible spring," the "day" issuing in declaring God's glory."

specific artifacts of creation, we have the opportunity to learn about the Designer and Creator. Romans 1:20 (NIV) reads, "For since the creation of the world God's invisible qualities—his eternal power and divine nature—have been clearly seen, being understood from what has been made, so that people are without excuse." So, what can we learn about God by observing His handiwork?

I love big trees. I have spent a few months recently in the Portland, Oregon area, and I am amazed at the tall redwoods, cedars, firs, and pines. But the most amazing trees I've seen are those in the Sequoia Tree National Forest in California. Sequoia trees, arguably the largest living organism on earth, send roots only twelve to fourteen feet deep even at maturity. A mature sequoia's roots can occupy over one acre of earth and contain over 90,000 cubic feet of soil.[23] They intertwine their roots with other sequoia trees so they can grow almost 300 feet tall. Giant sequoias are also one of the world's hardiest trees, living up to 3000 years. Their thick bark makes them flame resistant, as well as resistant to fungal rot and wood boring beetles. Their branches can be eight feet in diameter, and General Sherman, a giant sequoia, boasts a total volume of more than 52,000 cubic feet.[24]

What do these interesting facts tell us about the Designer and Creator? First, He is an amazing architect, able to design around the structural challenges to making a tree so large. Second, He is well aware of the threats to trees and designed this species so that it could live long enough to grow so large. Third, He loves diversity. The giant sequoia is only one of at least 60,000 different species of trees.[25]

---

23 Giant-sequoia.com. Accessed on 10/3/20 from: https://www.giant-sequoia.com/faqs/giant-sequoia-questions/
24 Tentree.com. Accessed on 10/3/20 from: https://www.tentree.com/blogs/posts/15-incredible-facts-about-giant-sequoia-trees
25 BBC.com. Accessed on 9/15/20 from: https://www.bbc.com/news/science-environment-39492977

What's Your Story?

On the other end of the size spectrum is the Pelagibacter Ubique. It is one of the smallest known free living (not dependent upon a host organism) bacteria, with a length of 370 to 890 nanometers and an average cell diameter of 120 to 200 nanometers.[26] A nanometer is one billionth of a meter or ten times smaller than the width of your DNA. Pelagibacter Ubique also has the smallest free living bacterium genome: 1.3 Mbp (One Mbp equals one million base pairs, a measure of the size of an individual gene within a DNA molecule),[27] 1354 protein genes, and thirty-five RNA genes. They are among the most common and smallest organisms in the ocean, with their total weight exceeding that of all of the fish in the sea!

What do I learn about God from the Pelagibacter Ubique? First, that even the smallest of God's creatures are very complex. This smallest known genome has 1.3 million base pairs. Given these observations, I am encouraged that He was able to design me to be just the man to tell my part of the story of God's glory. Second, that God's design includes features that to us may seem unimportant because of their small size, and yet in God's design, the Pelagibacter Ubique together form the largest portion of life in the oceans. Certainly, His ways are higher than our ways (Isa. 55:9)!

Each part of creation, each star, planet, and species is "telling" its unique part of the story of God's glory. The human race has its role in telling the story of God's glory, and within the story of humanity, we each have our unique part to play. What is the unique part of the human story assigned to you? Not one single part of the story, including yours, should be left out. How can you align your life, not just your

---

26 Microbewiki.kenyon.edu. Accessed on 9/15/20 from: https://microbewiki.kenyon.edu/index.php/Pelagibacter_ubique

27 Britanica.com. Accessed on 9/15/20 from: https://www.britannica.com/science/base-pair

religious or spiritual life, but your whole life with the story God created you to tell? The story will take some "back roads,"... but it is worth the telling.

Rediscovering Our Story

In 2 Kings 22, there is a story about a high priest named Hilkiah, who was commanded to oversee renovations in the temple. During the repairs, the Book of the Law was found. Apparently, the writings of Moses had been relegated to some dark corner and forgotten. When King Josiah learned about the contents of the book, he realized that for generations, they had gone astray, not following the Lord's commands. Because of King Josiah's response, it is clear that this discovery radically changed his view of who God is and his responsibilities as king.

We are living in a culture with competing worldviews. One view believes the narrative that out of nothingness, not even empty space, our universe emerged through the Big Bang, and all of life has since evolved through random mutations. The other view believes that God pre-existed creation and designed the universe and all of life to reveal His glory. One view says everything is random and has no objective purpose. The other says that everything was intelligently designed with a purpose in mind. Without purpose, there is nothing to fulfill.

In William Dembski's theory of intelligent design, if an event has a very small probability of occurring by chance and also meets the requirements of a prior specification, there is sufficient evidence of intelligent design rather than occurring by mere chance. Dembski defines "specification" as a pattern that holds meaning for the accomplishment of a purpose not yet fulfilled. Fulfillment results from meeting an already existing specification.[28] For instance, a string of letters

---

28 William Dembski, The Design Inference, Eliminating chance through

has meaning only if they form a word that already exists by a prior specification (e.g., a definition in the dictionary). Only then can that word fulfill the purpose of expressing the author's intended meaning.

Like King Josiah, whose world was shattered by the truth of God's word, we need to unlearn much that is believed and taught about the origin and nature of humans. Either we are products of meaningless randomness, or we are wonderfully and fearfully designed to fulfill our role in telling the story of God's glory. These two stories are incompatible. We must believe one and reject the other.

Does that mean we must reject science? Not at all! Instead, we must redeem it. Imre Lakatos, a widely quoted philosopher of science, proposed that all scientific theories begin with an apriori starting point that tends to resist all evidence to the contrary.[29] This apriori (i.e., prior to logic) starting point for a theory is not scientific in itself because it is assumed to be unquestionably true, not needing any evidence to support it. Believing that science must be at least agnostic in order to actually be science is one of the possible starting points to build a scientific theory. It is just as reasonable to begin scientific research from the starting point that God is there, and He has spoken.[30] And that is where this story begins.

Our Story Corrupted

If humans are the result of God's intelligent design, then according to Dembski's logic, there must have been a prior specification for human

---

small probabilities, (Cambridge, UK: Cambridge University Press, 1998), 3-5
29 Imre Lakatos, "Falsification and the methodology of scientific research programmes," In Imre Lakatos & Alan Musgrave (eds.), Criticism and the Growth of Knowledge (Cambridge, UK: Cambridge University Press, 1970), pp. 91–196.
30 Francis Schaeffer, He Is There and He Is Not Silent (Carol Stream, IL: Tyndale House Publishers,1972).

nature, which held meaning for the accomplishment of God's purposes.³¹ Put bluntly; God did not fiddle with the clay until He figured out what He wanted humans to be. He had in mind a specific purpose for the human race before He created us. God revealed that purpose in Genesis 1:26:

> Then God said, "Let us make man in our image, in our likeness, and let them rule (Hebrew: "radah") over the fish of the sea and the birds of the air, over the livestock, over all the earth, and over all the creatures that move along the ground."

God wanted to create a God-likeness to live on earth. Out of all of the characteristics that belong to God that He could have formed in us, He chose to have us represent Him as rulers. Ruling over our environment as God rules over all creation is the function we are to fulfill. It is our role in telling the story of God's glory.

However, a problem emerges from the typical dictionary definition of the Hebrew word "radah." Hebrew scholars define "radah" as ruling over other people, treading upon people or things, and persecuting one's enemies.³² In the Theological Dictionary of the Old Testament, Zoebel comments: "The prominent role of the root rdh (radah) in royal language explains both the use of the root for all kinds of supremacy and its frequent association with acts of violence, linked in part with the motif of anger."³³ At some point, ruling over our

---

31 William Dembski, The Design Inference, Eliminating chance through small probabilities (Cambridge, UK: Cambridge University Press, 1998), 3-5.

32 Francis Brown, S.R. Driver, and Charles Briggs, eds., A Hebrew and English Lexicon of the Old Testament. (Oxford, England: Clarendon Press, 1979) 921. William White, "Radah".in R. Laird Harris, Gleason Archer, and Bruce Waltke, eds., Theological Wordbook of the Old Testament (Chicago: Moody Press, 1980) 2:833.

33 Greifswald Zobel, "Radah" in Johannes Botterweck, Helmer Ringgren, Heiz-Josef Fabry, eds, Stott, D.W., Trans., Theological Dictionary of the

What's Your Story?

environment became ruling over, and even violently crushing, other people. What an inconceivable description of God's purpose for humanity! First, how could we all be rulers over other people? If some humans are rulers over humans, then the other humans are not rulers but the ruled. Second, it is contrary to the teachings of Jesus,

> Jesus called them together and said, "You know that those who are regarded as rulers of the Gentiles lord it over them, and their high officials exercise authority over them. Not so with you. Instead, whoever wants to become
>
> great among you must be your servant, and whoever wants to be first must be slave of all." (Mark 10:24-44 NIV)

And,

> Jesus said, "My kingdom is not of this world. If it were, my servants would fight to prevent my arrest by the Jewish leaders. But now my kingdom is from another place." (John 18:36 NIV)

In defense of these scholars' work, their proposed meanings of the Hebrew radah were obtained through the normal strategy to define a word from the context in every occurrence in the Hebrew scriptures. However, included in this survey are post-fall examples that reveal sin's corruption of man's ruling. The following are some examples:

> I will set my face against you so that you will be defeated by your enemies; those who hate you will rule (radah) over you, and you will flee even when no one is pursuing you. (Leviticus 26:17)

> You have not strengthened the weak or healed the sick or bound up the injured. You have not brought back the strays or searched for the lost. You have ruled (radah) them harshly and brutally. (Ezekiel 34:4)

Old Testament (Grand Rapids: Wm.B. Eerdmans Publishing, 2001) 13:333.

But as soon as they were at rest, they again did what was evil in your sight. Then you abandoned them to the hand of their enemies so that they ruled over (radah) them. (Nehemiah 9:28)

It seems that God's meaning of "radah" before humanity's fall must have differed from how people began to rule after the emergence of our sinful nature. Humans were originally to rule over "the fish of the sea and the birds of the air, over the livestock, over all the earth, and over all the creatures that move along the ground." It was only after the fall that the word "radah" came to mean dominating other humans. The concept that God's original purpose in creating humans was that they should violently dominate other humans is repugnant. We need to rethink the strategy for discovering the meaning of "radah" in the context of Genesis one.

Is this issue still relevant to us? Have humans even retained the capacity to "radah" even though we miss the mark of God's intention? Is it still possible for us to be rulers over our environment as God intended?

Theologians have wrestled for centuries with the meaning of being created in the "image of God." That discussion is long and leads to many nuanced concepts that are beyond the scope of this book. Evangelical scholars have concluded that the image of God exists formally in our personality (moral responsibility and intelligence) and materially in our knowledge of God and His will for us. Essentially, the image of God was not destroyed by Adam's fall but rather distorted.[34] By giving us intelligence and moral responsibility, God designed us to do something intelligently but also with moral integrity. We were created to imitate Him in some important ways, and we still can do that to

---

34 Carl Henry, "Image of God," in Walter Elwell, ed., Evangelical Dictionary of Theology, (Grand Rapids, MI: Baker Book House, 1984) 547.

some extent, but because of our sin, we tend to do it for our glory instead of God's.[35]

So, are we still destined to rule over our environment, or has this purpose been forever lost? Apostle John gives us the answer to this last question in the final chapter of the book of Revelation,

> No longer will there be any curse. The throne of God and of the Lamb will be in the city, and his servants will serve him. They will see his face, and his name will be on their foreheads. There will be no more night. They will not need the light of a lamp or the light of the sun, for the Lord God will give them light. And they will reign forever and ever. (Revelation 22:3-5 NIV)

Humanity was both initially created to rule and ultimately will be redeemed from sin to reign with Christ forever and ever. So, being the image of the Ruling God was our story before the fall, and after redemption is completed, it will be our story for eternity. However, learning how to rule the same way God rules is also our story as we live out the redemption of this God-likeness. A theology of redemption that ignores the redemption of our ruling would be incomplete.

Redefining What it Means to Rule

Perhaps the best approach for defining "radah" as God originally intended comes from the context of the creation story in Genesis. When God decided to create humans in His image, He went beyond just displaying what He could do; He chose to reveal a particular part of His character. After saying, "Let us make man in our image, in our likeness," He could have said, "and let them love." Or He could have

---

[35] Derek Kidner, Genesis, An introduction and commentary. (Downers Grove, IL: Intervarsity Press, 1967) 73.

said, "and let them speak the truth." Instead, God said, "and let them rule." Certainly, God wants us to speak the truth in love, but when God wanted to represent His image and likeness on earth, He created rulers. We were created not only to be like God but also to, in some small way, do what God does.

So, what specifically was God doing that we were to imitate? Genesis one reveals that God created the heavens and the earth through two distinct and separate processes: separating and filling. God separates things to create order and then fills them with meaning, purpose, and value. Note the following examples of each:

Separating:

...and he separated the light from the darkness (v. 4)

...and separated the water under the expanse from the water above it (v. 6)

...and let the water under the sky be gathered to one place, and let the dry ground appear (v. 9)

...Let there be lights in the expanse of the sky to separate the day from the night (v. 14)

...and to separate light from darkness (v. 18)

Filling:

...Let the land produce vegetation (v. 11)

...Let the water teem with living creatures (v. 20)

...Be fruitful and increase in number and fill the water in the seas, and let the birds increase on the earth (v. 22)

...Let the land produce living creatures according to their kinds (v. 24-25)

God filled His creation with meaning. In Genesis 1:14-15, God reveals that the "lights in the vault of the sky [are to] serve as signs to mark sacred times, and days and years, and let them be lights in the vault of the sky to give light on the earth." The land, sea, and air were filled with vegetation, animals, fish, and birds to form ecosystems that would be interdependent and would provide a context in which Adam could rule.

God also filled His creation with purpose. Each time God separated chaos into order, He progressively prepared distinct parts of creation to function as He intended. In other words, the goal was not simply to create a distance between the waters above from the waters below or the waters from the dry ground, but God was creating an order that specifically prepared each part of creation for the filling He had planned. Heavy fog is not fit for fish or fowl. It had to be separated into the sea and the sky to create a suitable habitat for each.

Additionally, God gave meaning to His creation by giving it names. God called the light "day" and the darkness "night." God called the expanse above the water "sky." God called the dry ground "land" and the gathered waters "seas." Later in one of Adam's first training sessions on how to rule, God let Adam name the animals. (Genesis 2:19-20) Naming things is how we associate a person, place, thing, or event with meaning. It is also one way we form a relationship and express what it means to us. The privilege of naming something generally goes to its creator or discoverer. It is also one way we claim ownership of something and assume the right to rule over it.

Finally, God filled His creation with value. Five of the six days of creation contained God's proclamation, "It was good." It was not until He assessed His creation of Adam that God said, "It is not good for the man to be alone." These are value judgments. Value is based on purpose and/or meaning. Something has instrumental value if it will assist in the accomplishment of a purpose. That's why I value my tools. Having the right tool for the job makes it easier to get the results I want.

Something has emotional value if it helps us form or maintain our identity. We form our sense of who we are typically based on the roles we fulfill. If you were asked to stand and introduce yourself to a group of strangers, you might give your name, occupation, city of residence, etc. Your name represents your family heritage. Your occupation represents not only your accomplishments, but also something you have been passionate about enough in which to invest your "blood, sweat, and tears." We also attach emotional value to the things that remind us of our past (e.g. old photos and childhood toys), which is part of who we are.

God decided that His creation was valuable for displaying His glory. It had both instrumental and emotional value to God. However, Adam was not able to fully be the God-likeness on earth until God created Eve. The value of human life is not based on their contribution to society or their lifelong earning potential, but it is based on being the God-likeness on earth to tell the story of God's glory. But God is very specific on how He wants us to tell that story.

Following this marvelous demonstration of separating and filling, God created Adam and Eve in His image, and as part of that image, He blessed them with a function to fulfill.[36]

> Be fruitful and increase in number; fill the earth and subdue it. Rule ("radah") over the fish of the sea and the birds of the air and over every living creature that moves on the ground."
> (Gen 1:28)

Wenham commented on this blessing/command given to Adam and Eve, "Because man is created in God's image, he is king over nature. He rules the world on God's behalf. Ruling over our environment, however, is no license for the unbridled exploitation and subjugation

---

[36] Derek Kidner, Genesis, An introduction and commentary. (Downers Grove, IL: Intervarsity Press, 1967), 52.

of nature. Ancient oriental kings were expected to be devoted to the welfare of their subjects."[37]

The phrase "Be fruitful and increase in number" modifies the phrase "fill the earth." Being fruitful expresses the idea of procreation, literally to fill the earth with people. However, the connection between being fruitful and "subduing the earth" is less obvious. The increase in population would fulfill physically "filling the earth," but "subduing it" does not. Subduing must be a different responsibility and has to do with a particular type of separating.

If God provided the model by separating and filling the cosmos, why did He commission us to fill and subdue? A partial explanation could be to express the difference between simply choosing to view something as being separate and actually separating things in our environment. When God separates, it makes a difference "out there." It produces objective results, not just subjective ones that are a mere matter of perspective. God's "radah" begins with a command to force His will upon the formless and empty darkness. We find God as the "first cause," forcing order upon the chaos in each successive step.[38] So to subdue the earth, as God subdued creation, means we must make a difference beyond ourselves. But, on what difference should we focus? God will call and gift each believer to make their unique contribution; however, the primary goal should always be that God is glorified. We are to build his kingdom, not ours. His kingdom is made up of people who not only believe in and follow Him but also rule over their environment like Him.

---

[37] Gordon Wenham, Word Biblical Commentary, Vol. 1, Genesis 1-15 (Waco, TX: Word Books, 1987) 1:33.
[38] Genesis 1:2 The earth was formless and void. The Hebrew word for "formless" (tohu) can be translated as "chaos"

First and foremost, we need to cooperate with God to bring order and fullness into our relationship with God, to others' relationship to God, and to our relationships with each other. However, we also need to bring order (e.g., truth and integrity) and fullness (e.g., meaning, purpose, and value) to our environment, including our marriages, our homes, our economy, our politics, our legal system, our education system, our media, the arts, etc. This is not an either/or proposition. We do not have to choose between either a spiritual or social gospel. Instead, we need to let the Holy Spirit work in us so that our God-like ruling is transformed to be salt and light to our broken world.

Ruling Like God Rules

Creating an orderly and full world was not the only possible type of subduing God could have done. Instead of creating order out of the chaos, God could have subdued creation by destroying it or simply discarding it. Like a vandal, he could have even defaced it by adding to its chaos, or more radically emptying it of any future potential by destroying it. But that is not the character of God. He created order out of chaos and filled the newly ordered part of creation with meaning, purpose, and value.

Separating and filling were also not the only possible ways to create order. God could have blended the elements into a homogeneous soup with each element perfectly distributed so that any measured volume of the soup would yield the same analysis as any other sample. However, a creation that lacked uniqueness would be inconsistent with the character of God, who is glorified by the unimaginable diversity we see in nature.

The third relationship between God-like separation and subduing is found in the reason why God created: to reveal the majesty of His glory (Psalm 19). For our separating to reveal the glory of God, these processes must produce outward, visible results. That does not mean that all separating is external, but that in the end, like saving faith, it produces outward evidence of our inner character.

The inner character of those who subdue is revealed by what, how, and why they chose to subdue. Our ruling was never intended to place one person in authority over other people, but rather, we were intended to rule collectively over our environment. Likewise, our ruling was never intended to exploit nature but to care for it. Caring for nature, however, does not mean, as some presume, that nature should be left alone. That would be an abdication of our reign. Before the fall, God assigned Adam to till, or cultivate, and guard the garden (Gen 2:15). Wenham comments on the word translated "till" in this verse, "[It] is a very common verb and is often used of cultivating the soil (2:5, 3:23, 4:2, 12, etc.)."[39] Adam's responsibility to till the garden implies that it would not stay fruitful without Adam's subduing it.

The corruption of sin, however, has led humans to violently subdue each other, resulting in God having to create ruling structures in society. God instituted human government to protect human life through God's covenant with Noah (Gen 9:1-17), and the monarchy was granted to Israel when they rejected God as their king (1 Samuel 8:1-9). Still, David's throne has been given to the Lamb of God so that when sin is finished, all humanity will reign with Christ in submission to God (Revelations 22:5).

But, simply creating order was not sufficient to display God's glory. Order alone is sterile and unfulfilling. After creating order through separation, God completed the process by filling. "Malae" (to fill) conveys the idea of making something or someone complete.[40] Certainly,

---

39 Gordon Wenham, Word Biblical Commentary, Vol. 1, Genesis 1-15 (Waco, TX: Word Books, 1987) 1:33.
40 Snijders, L.A, (1997). "malae," in Johannes Botterweck, Helmer Ring-

its meaning includes the idea of being fruitful through procreation from the parallelism in Genesis 1:28 and also in the command to the animals (Gen 1:22). However, if we once again use the model of God in creation, "radah" expresses much more than this.

Notice the process that God goes through in each step of filling His creation. First, the process began with ascribing purpose to the chaos and emptiness. This was done through the design that specified the separation of creation into a purposeful order. Once the order was established, then the emptiness was ready to be filled. In Genesis one, the things to be filled were first set in order or prepared for their ultimate purpose. For example, the water and the dry land were separated before either was filled. Until separated, the silt-filled water was not an acceptable habitat for either fish or land animals.

Second, as part of the filling process, God named each newly ordered part of His creation. Why was it necessary to name the dry ground, the gathered waters, or any other part of creation for that matter? What purpose was accomplished by giving unique names to things? The answer is not that God needs names by which to reference each part. God has a much more intimate knowledge of His creation than simply through its names. God alone didn't need names, but God in communion with humans would. Names were needed later when God would have someone with whom He could communicate about His creation. In other words, filling includes not only imparting purpose to a thing but also ascribing meaning.

Third, meaning was given to specific parts of His new creation through the unique purpose given it. Genesis 1:14-18 reads,

---

gren, Heiz-Josef Fabry, eds, Douglas Stott, trans., Theological Dictionary of the Old Testament (Grand Rapids, MI: W.B. Eerdmans Publishing Co., 2001)

What's Your Story?

"And God said, "Let there be lights in the vault of the sky to separate the day from the night, and let them serve as signs to mark sacred times, and days and years, and let them be lights in the vault of the sky to give light on the earth." And it was so. God made two great lights—the greater light to govern the day and the lesser light to govern the night. He also made the stars. God set them in the vault of the sky to give light on the earth, to govern the day and the night, and to separate light from darkness.

Notice that the sun and moon were to "serve as signs to mark sacred times and days and years." So the sun and moon were to hold meaning concerning the passage of time. Meaning and purpose are closely linked. As someone or something accomplishes a purpose, it has implications (i.e., meaning) for all those affected by the change produced by accomplishing the purpose. Day and night each have a different meaning for us (i.e., they hold different implications for us) because God created the sun and moon to "separate the light from the darkness."

Meaning is also grounded in relationships, often the relationships of creation and ownership. Psalm 74:16 says, "The day is yours, and yours also the night; you established the sun and moon." Since God created the sun and moon, He owns both the sun and moon and their effects (i.e., day and night). For example, I prefer to make Christmas gifts whenever possible. I find particular joy in transforming wood into Christmas tree ornaments, fruit bowls, sculptures, etc. The end product means much more than what it would sell for. It represents not only my time and skills but also the design reflects my particular creative style. There is a special bond between the craftsman and His creations. How much more so when we procreate. Our child is not just "a baby" but "my baby." We have special emotional attachments to those whom we conceive and birth. So too, God assumed ownership of all that He created and ascribed every part of it as holding meaning as a demonstration of His glory (Psalm 19, Romans 1:20).

The concept of meaning is defined in two ways, first, as a spatial relationship between two sets in which corresponding elements can be mapped.[41] Think of a spatial relationship like a location within a context. At the time of writing this, I live in Kansas, but of course, that also means I live in the United States and in North America. I also have some very close relationships and other relationships that are more distant. The character of my various relationships can be mapped based on the level of meaning of those relationships to me.

Second, meaning is also defined as a functional relationship in which one element instrumentally affects change in the other's behavior.[42] As I mentioned above, the accomplishment of a purpose has implications (i.e., meaning) for all those affected by the change produced by accomplishing the purpose. Those implications hold the type of meaning based on a functional relationship. During the summer, when the sun shines and summer storms water the ground, my grass grows. This means I will have to mow the lawn. When my bank balance gets low, it means I will need to slow down my spending. Think of a functional relationship as a change in one thing that causes, or at least implies a need for, a change in something else.

Third, when God had filled the darkness with light, the seas teeming with fish, the night sky with stars, and the earth with every living thing, He saw that it was good. Ascribing value is the final act in the process of filling. God did not call anything good until it was separat-

---

41 Fauconnier, G. (1997). Mappings in Thought and Language. Cambridge, England: Cambridge University Press.
42 Daniel Dennett, Brainstorms, Philosophical Essays on Mind and Psychology, (Cambridge, MA: The MIT Press, 1978), 80.

ed and filled. Value is determined by the sum of purpose and meaning. The value I place on anything is factored by the degree to which it aligns with my purpose(s) and by my personal investment in it, or my desire for it, which is to say, its meaning to me. Therefore, as each part of creation is made to properly align with God's purpose through His own handiwork, it receives value.

When something is full, God calls it good. In this sense, fullness is a synonym for goodness. The relationship between fullness and goodness (and also beauty) is evident throughout the Scriptures. Consider the following brief list of examples:

1. The Promised Land was described as flowing (over full) with milk and honey (Exodus 3:8)
2. The blessings of God included a full life (Exodus 23:25-26)
3. Joseph's children were blessed with the best gifts of the earth and its fullness (Deuteronomy 33:16)
4. You make known to me the path of life; you will fill me with joy in your presence (Psalm 16:11)
5. The earth is the Lord's and all the fullness thereof. (Psalm 24:1)
6. The church is described as the fullness of Jesus who fills everything in every way (Ephesians 1:23)
7. Paul's prayer for the Ephesians was that they might be filled to the measure of all the fullness of God (Ephesians 3:19)
8. The goal of spiritual growth is described as attaining to the whole measure of the fullness of Christ (Ephesians 4:13)
9. Paul urges the Ephesians to be filled with the Spirit (literally: constantly being kept filled) (Ephesians 5:18)
10. God was pleased to have all His fullness dwell in Christ (Colossians 1:19)
11. Believers have been given fullness in Christ (Colossians 2:10)

The opposite is also true. Emptiness is equated with worthlessness and disgrace:
1. Naomi laments that God had brought her back from Moab empty (Ruth 1:21)
2. God does not listen to empty pleas (Job 35:13)
3. God's word does not return to Him empty (Isaiah 55:11)
4. Rebellious Israel was described as an empty vine (Hosea 10:1)
5. God redeemed us from an empty way of life (I Peter 1:18)

From the creation story, we can now outline the meaning of "radah" as it was modeled by God as follows:

"radah" involves two processes:
1. Subduing, including: separating chaos into a purposeful order forcing your will upon something to align it with God's purpose
2. Filling, including:
   ascribing meaning
   ascribing purpose
   ascribing value

Given the above, Genesis 1:26-28 reveals we were created to glorify God by ruling over the earth and all it contains by separating and filling our environment. Fulfillment does not come from building an earthly "kingdom" for our own glory. No matter how rich, powerful, famous, admired, credentialed, or in any other way we are successful, we will only be fulfilled once we submit to ruling over the realms given us within the Kingdom of God for the glory of God. Only then will we each reveal to the rest of creation our unique part in the story of the glory of God and finally find rest in true fulfillment.

What's Your Story?

Discussion Questions

1. What unique story of the glory of God's grace does your life tell?

2. What are some ways in your job or home responsibilities that you create order by separating them?

   a. Separating things physically (like separating dirt from laundry by washing it.)

   b. Separating things mentally (like putting information or data into different categories)

3. What are some ways in your job or home responsibilities that you create meaning to things or that you change or add to things, to make them more meaningful?

   a. Adding spatial meaning can be physical (e.g., literally putting things closer together), procedural (e.g., adjusting the order in which things happen), or emotional (e.g., establishing an emotional bond with someone or something).

b. Adding functional meaning results from increasing the usefulness of someone (as in teaching them a new skill) or something (as in refining a raw material or interpreting raw data)

4. What part of your job or home responsibilities requires you to create new goals or purposes?

5. What is one or two examples of what you do at home or in your job that creates value for others?

4

King Adam Before and After His Fall

Now that we have identified the processes of separating and filling as God's strategy to rule over His creation, we have a problem. Humans don't appear to consistently rule in the same way God ruled over creation. If God's ruling over creation is to be the model for the God-like ruling of humans, then there needs to be evidence that before his rebellion, Adam was ruling by using the same processes as God. Was Adam separating to create order and filling his environment with meaning, purpose, and value? This leads us to the question: "In what way does Adam demonstrate being the image of the Ruler-God before the fall?" The God-like man was to represent God on the earth by ruling ("radah") over "the fish of the sea and the birds of the air and over every living creature that moves on the ground." To support the validity of the view that separating and filling were to be Adam's outworking of his God-likeness, we would need evidence of him separating and filling before his nature was corrupted by the fall. Does God give him tasks to do that require him to separate and fill? Does Adam naturally respond to his circumstances by separating and filling?

We only have two recorded activities of the Pre-fall Adam; however, it is significant that each of them illustrates a unique part of "radah." Genesis 2:15 states, "The Lord took the man and put him in the Garden of Eden to work it and take care of it." There has been much speculation as to the specific activities implied in this assignment. Did he plow and plant as we conceive agricultural work? Adam certainly did not need to weed the garden because weeds (thorns and thistles) did not appear until after the curse upon the ground. Nor did he water the garden because God had already provided for this through subterranean streams (Gen 2:6).

Although we do not know the specifics of Adam's responsibilities, we can interpret their function from the two words used to describe them. First, Adam was to work or cultivate ("abad") the garden. Walter Kaiser notes that in reference to things, "abad" is usually followed by an accusation of the thing upon which the labor is expended, e.g., "to till" a field; "to dress" a vineyard.[43] The implication is that the one whose work effects a change upon the object of their labor. The word "abad" is used in Genesis 2:15 to describe Adam's purpose, and includes the concept of cultivating or in some way making the plants in the garden subservient to him.[44] In some sense, God wanted Adam to express his will toward the garden and to cause the desired changes to occur.

Second, Adam was responsible to take care of ("shamar") the garden. According to Hartley, "shamar" refers to watching over, pro-

---

43 Walter Kaiser, "abad," in R. Laird Harris, Gleason Archer, and Bruce Waltke, eds., Theological Wordbook of the Old Testament, (Chicago: Moody Press, 1980), 2:639-641.
44 C.F. Keil and F. Delitzsch (1978). The Pentateuch, in Commentary on the Old Testament, James Martin, Tr. Grand Rapids, MI: W.B. Eerdmans. Vol. 1, p. 84

tecting, and preserving.[45] Most words were originally pictographs and then metaphors.[46] To be "tied up" generally means in our culture that you are unavailable due to other commitments. Originally the phrase was a metaphor that compared being bound by ropes to being too busy to accept additional commitments. Included in the word picture of "shamar" is the establishment of a perimeter with a hedge and then patrolling the perimeter to keep watch. The implication was that God was warning Adam of a future attack upon the garden. How sad that Adam's "shamar" did not successfully defend them from Satan's lies and half-truths. God designed Adam to "radah" over Eden by forcing his will upon it and by keeping it separate from Satan's rebellion. Both "abad" and "shamar" are certainly in harmony with the concept of ruling over one's environment.

The other revealed activity of the Pre-fall Adam involves both separating and filling. God judged that it was not good for man to be alone. Although God obviously knew from the beginning how He would meet this need, He first took Adam through the process of naming the animals (Gen 2:18-20). Adam was beginning to separate, or distinguish between, the different species and to fill his world with meaning. In order to communicate with God, Adam needed language, and language needs nouns – like the names of things.

This activity, however, was more than just the classification of the various types of animals. The naming of the animals also provided the opportunity for Adam to perceive the separation that God had made between man and all other living creatures. The process concluded when Adam discovered there was no animal suitable as a companion

---

45 Herman Austel, "shamar," in R. Laird Harris, Gleason Archer, and Bruce Waltke, eds., Theological Wordbook of the Old Testament, (Chicago: Moody Press, 1980), 2:939-940.
46 A.T. Robertson (1930) Word Pictures in the New Testament. Nashville, TN: Broadman Press. preface X.

for him. So, God separated Eve out of Adam, and he found that she fulfilled his need for companionship. And what did Adam do? He named her. That is, he ascribed to her meaning (bone of my bone and flesh of my flesh), purpose (as a companion in separating and filling Adam's environment), and value (Adam's choice over the rest of creation).

Of course, Adam's naming of Eve does not imply ownership any more than his naming of the animals meant that he owned them either. Adam was just continuing with the previous process of naming the things God brought to him. Ascribing meaning and purpose to someone or something only means that we state our vision for the future even though we have no power to make that future a reality. Parents can give their children beautiful and positive names but that does not assure for them a beautiful or positive life. However, note that Adam's name for Eve held both spatial meaning (closeness to me, part of me) and functional meaning (companion in separating and filling his environment).

Adam was ruling over his environment as God's image on earth. He was simply acting as he had been designed. Note that the result of Adam's ruling was that he learned more about himself, his environment, and God's character. He learned that he was incomplete and needed a helper. He discovered no animal could help him rule, and third, he needed Eve to complete his God-likeness on earth. The result was Adam's joy over his new companion and helper.

Everything we have found in the pre-fall Adam suggests that he was designed and nurtured by God to separate and fill his environment. Separating requires that we exert our will upon our environment to create order. Adam's "abad" produced an effect upon the garden. Adam also separated himself from the animals and then filled Eve with meaning, purpose, and value. Therefore, as sons of Adam and daughters of Eve, we are also specifically designed to separate our environment and then fill it with meaning, purpose, and value for the glory of our Creator.

Because Eve was provided to help Adam rule, it should be noted that they formed a team to rule together over their environment. Much more about this will be discussed in chapter nine, but it needs to be said that ruling is not personally controlling others but rather using your influence. Each member of a successful team contributes their unique influence to affect the outcome. In that sense, they share a realm of responsibility. In this way, we share the ruling of many different realms with other people as we cooperate with them toward a goal. In practical application, we rarely rule in isolation from others.

Of course, the order and fullness that Adam had created would not last. The garden came under attack by the enemy of truth, the father of lies. The failure of Adam to protect the order and fullness of the garden led him to desire to blur the difference between himself and God; to be God instead of a God-likeness. In doing so, he emptied God's words of their meaning and chose to believe the enemy's lie. And so, Adam and Eve were emptied. They were emptied of their self-esteem, emptied of their confidence in God's love, and emptied of their freedom in the garden. They were ashamed, afraid of God, and trapped in their hiding place.

The Downward Spiral into Emptiness

God had created a perfectly ordered cosmos that was bubbling with meaning to tell the story of God's glory, uniquely designed for this purpose, and proclaimed to be "very good" (Gen 1:31). Then, through the choices Adam and Eve made, this orderly cosmos started to become more and more chaotic until, at last, they became empty of the God-likeness they were designed to be.

Kings and Queens in the Kingdom of God

To follow the progressive steps of this downward spiral into emptiness will first require examining some of the characteristics of the order God had created. What makes something ordered? What kinds of ordered cosmos could He have created?

First, His creation had categories. Members of a category share some characteristic that qualifies them to belong to that category. Of course, individuals belong to many overlapping categories. For instance, I belong to the category of all those who are male. I also belong to the categories of those who have gray hair, those who live in Kansas, have a Ph.D., teach at a Christian college, and who are writing a book. There are also more general categories (e.g., those who are male) and progressively more specific categories until only a single individual belongs to that category (e.g., the husband of Debbie Routon White).

Have you ever played 20 questions? It begins with someone identifying in their mind a particular individual person or thing. The first of the 20 questions is always, "Is it animal, vegetable, or mineral?" These are the most general categories. After that, all questions must be answered with a "yes," or "no." If the answer is "animal," then you might overlay an intersecting category by asking, "Is he or she human?" and then, "Is he or she alive?" Each question searches for another overlapping category to which the mystery thing or person belongs. The goal of the game is before asking the 20th question to multiply the possible overlapping categories until at the intersection of all these categories, only one particular person or thing belongs to all of the listed categories.

God created categories such as angels, humans, birds, fish, plants bearing seeds, trees bearing fruit, livestock, creatures that move along the ground, and wild animals. Within each of these general categories, He created "each according to their kinds." Within these "kinds," biologists have identified more specific categories such as phylum, class, order, family, genus, and species progressively. Then, within each species, there are individuals who are all a little bit different from each other. When considering the vast number of plant and animal species and the uniqueness of each individual plant, animal, or human, it is evident that God loves diversity!

Everything that God separated created a new category. Satan's lies have, in part, attempted to blur the separation between these categories. His temptation of Eve was that she could become like God, knowing right from wrong. Satan's goal was to break down the categorical difference between himself (a fallen angel) and Adam so that Adam would also fall. Satan desires to destroy the order of God's creation by blending categories to create chaos. The boundaries God created to define categories, Satan works to destroy.

Second, God created institutions. Institutions have institutes or laws. Interestingly, one of the first institutions God created eventually developed into the process of science. He did this by having Adam name the animals, compare them to himself, and discover their level of fitness as a helper for him. This search for truth through observation followed the rules of purposeful research, adequate sampling size, and a conclusion based upon the observation data. This process then led to the creation of Eve and the institution of marriage with its rules: "a man leaves his father and mother and is united to his wife, and they become one flesh" (Gen 2:24). Some of the other institutions that God created were work (Gen 2:15), human government (Gen 9:5-6), education (Exodus 18:20, Deuteronomy 4:1-10), and the church (Acts 2).

Another of Satan's strategies is to destroy the institutions that God created. His lies attempt to change the rules and create new categories. He urges us to make decisions solely on our feelings or perhaps political optics. He tries to convince us that stealing from the company is ok because they pay you so little, and that you can be an effective Christian without being involved with any particular church. The institution of marriage has been blurred so now sustained cohabitation is considered essentially the same as marriage. We have had to create new categories such as "significant other," "baby momma," and "baby daddy."

Third, God created relationships between the categories within the institutions. The Enemy loves to destroy relationships because that is how he can get us to deface God's institutions. One way that he destroys relationships is through the blurring of the separation between categories. When a man is married, he is to separate himself from any sexual intimacy with every woman other than his wife. But Satan will feed him the lie that if his wife doesn't meet his sexual needs, he is free to find them elsewhere. The enemy will convince church elders that putting on appearances (i.e., a fake or partial repentance) is acceptable when a full, true repentance seems too hard. He will also tempt coworkers to undercut each other in their scramble for a promotion. In other words, the enemy whispers lies to us to get us to believe there are "grey areas" between right and wrong that aren't as bad as the bold "black" wrong. These "grey areas' are usually just our rationalizations to help us feel better about what we plan to do.

A category is simply a description of a characteristic shared by all of its members. Categories can be true descriptions of boundaries between different groups in God's reality. Categories can also be created in the perceptions of humans that may or may not align with God's categorization. Some categories describe our nature, such as being human. Our behavior and the conditions caused by our behavior can also place us in a category. Therefore some categories we belong to can change as a result of our behaviors. (Once I was single, now I am married) I belong to many different categories (married, old, educated,

King Adam Before and After His Fall

a sinner saved by grace), but my supposed membership in a category depends on who is categorizing me. To categorize someone or something is to ascribe meaning, purpose, and value to them. We are doing God-like ruling when we categorize someone or something into the same categories that God places them. In other words, when we value them as God values them for the same reason that God values them.

It did not take long in the Genesis account for categories to be merged, institutions to break down, and relationships to crumble. Adam blamed Eve for his choice, and so trust in the first marriage was broken. Cain destroyed his family relationships by killing his brother. In just seven generations, Lamech twisted marriage into polygamy and justice into revenge (Gen 4:18-24). Eventually, God saw that "every inclination of the thoughts of the human heart was only evil all the time" (Gen 6:5) and planned to empty the earth of humanity. Apostle Paul summarized this downward spiral in Romans 1:21-25 and 3:12,

> For although they knew God, they neither glorified him as God nor gave thanks to him, but their thinking became futile, and their foolish hearts were darkened. Although they claimed to be wise, they became fools and exchanged the glory of the immortal God for images made to look like a mortal human being and birds and animals and reptiles. Therefore, God gave them over in the sinful desires of their hearts to sexual impurity for the degrading of their bodies with one another. They exchanged the truth about God for a lie and worshipped and served created things rather than the Creator—who is forever praised. All have turned away; they have together become worthless.

The downward spiral began when, in pride, they claimed to be wise. Unwilling to accept the category of being made in God's image and the rules associated with being creations of God, they chose to rebel from that category and create the new category of "creators of new gods." The result of rejecting the One who created them was that God released them to continue in their self-made downward spiral. So, they chose to also rebel against the created categories of male and female and the rules associated with the institution of marriage. In doing so, they found themselves in the chaos of a life without meaning (exchanged the truth for a lie), purpose (worshiping false gods), and value (… "they have together become worthless").

Yet, despite having lost the order of God's categories and institutions, humans have continued to reflect the image of God by being "hardwired" to separate and fill their environment. However, because they build on shifting sand instead of the Rock, generation after generation discovers at the end of their lives that they have ultimately failed to find meaning in life. Still, they keep on building. They keep trying to create their own meaning, purpose, and value. Or else, they would have no hope.

Today's Fallen God-like Rulers

Through the establishment of the new category of those who believe the Father who sent him (John 5:24) and the new institution of the church (Acts 2), God provided salt and light to our fallen world to restore His categories, institutions, and through them restore human relationships. However, in the past few decades, we have seen the influence of the church wane in America, and many of these categories and institutions attacked. Gender, marriage, and the family have been emptied of their biblical meaning. The institution of work—to provide for yourself and others through labor—is increasingly being rejected and replaced by dependency upon the government to provide for us through strategies for wealth redistribution. Even the category of humanness is being redefined from those created by God to bear

King Adam Before and After His Fall

His image to those who have evolved from the cosmic accident that somehow produced life. Increasingly, to be valued as a human, we must be wanted after we are born, not too expensive or difficult to care for, and beneficial to those who have political power. Ultimately, the value of human life has been reduced to our lifetime earning capacity rather than the degree to which we reflect God's image.

To be fulfilled, we must again realign ourselves with God's created categories and restore the institutions He established. We must return to being God-like rulers. Only then will we experience the fulfillment of bringing glory to God as He intended.

We need to reject the lies of the enemy who wants to rob God of the glory He might receive through us. One of Satan's lies comes in the form of secularism—narrowing God's Kingdom to "religious activities." This lie has been around for a long time, but it has recently become conventional wisdom in our secular society. Politicians and the press often criticize politicians or judges who would dare bring their faith into their policymaking or legal judgments. Secularists claim that religion should be private and have no influence in the public sphere. This secularization of society has led many Christians to compartmentalize their religious life (Sunday mornings) from the rest of their life (school, work, finances, friendships, etc.).

Patrick, the unfulfilled accountant, needs to escape this secular perspective and see that his accounting creates order out of the chaos of raw data. His value to the company, and one of the ways he glorifies God, is by filling the numbers with meaning. When he resists pressure from the management to creatively bury information from the stockholders or the IRS, he reflects the God-likeness created in him by separating himself from those who twist the truth for personal gain. Patrick also needs an enlarged vision of kingdom living that encompasses all of life and how his accounting career can enable him to contribute his spiritual gifts and time to building God's kingdom. That doesn't necessarily mean he has to be an accountant for a church or mission agency. Patrick's accounting job might be God's strategy for him to be salt and light to people with whom he would not otherwise have the opportunity to develop a relationship. By doing his job with excellence, having a positive attitude toward the challenges in the workplace, and being respectful of others, he can become a positive witness of what Christians are like. He can be an accountant and a valued employee for the glory of God!

Another of Satan's favorite lies is materialism – seeking fulfillment in things, but more specifically, the power to control our future, to be the "captain of our ship." Materialism is the natural extension of secularism because once you reject spiritual reality, then all you have left is a bunch of stuff and the power to control whatever you have collected. The enemies of God know that our sinful nature craves to fill our emptiness with consumption. But beyond seeking to live comfortably in this physical world, philosophical materialism is also an attempt to find meaning and purpose in a world without consequences. If there is no God, there is no basis for ethics, therefore materialists use their "good works" to justify whatever they deem necessary to achieve their goals.

Secular scientists routinely run into data that would logically lead to the conclusion of intelligent design. However, as committed philosophic materialists, and therefore must assume that everything that exists is the result of chance and natural causes, they must search for a different answer, no matter how contorted that answer might be. Why? Simply because if there is an Intelligent Designer, he would be more powerful than us and might destroy us. Goodbye to our ability to control our future. We would be vulnerable, and that would be unthinkable. Literally unthinkable!

King Adam Before and After His Fall

However, most people in our culture are not thinking about the implications of Intelligent Design. They only want to earn more, buy more, and store more. We are like the man in Jesus' parable whose solution to harvesting too much grain for his barns to hold was to build bigger barns (Luke 12:13-21). This man turned from believing in God's providence, and he put his faith for his future in the accumulation of material things. Francis Schaeffer pointed out that the opposite of materialism is not poverty but "compassionate use of accumulated wealth."[47] Jesus called the man in this parable a fool, not because he was rich in material things, but because he was NOT rich toward God.

Susan, the online business owner, needs to understand that increasing their income beyond their current lifestyle, for one thing, ignores the greater need for God's love and mercy in her community. Making more money to buy more stuff and take expensive vacations will not bring her the level of fulfillment she desires. Of course, these things will bring her enjoyment, but creating order and beauty in small levels of chaos brings small levels of fulfillment. Suppose Susan took the time to become aware of the hurting people and the injustice in her community. She might see that by volunteering to use her spiritual gifts to minister to her community and contribute to the needs she encounters, she would help change lives and the lives that these changed people eventually will impact. That would be creating an immense level of order and value, and with it, a deep sense of fulfillment.

Humanism, another lie straight from the pit, is similar to materialism in one way. It is yet another strategy to control our future. Humanists trust that through self-improvement, they can create a better future for themselves and others. They believe that humans are essentially

---

47 Francis Schaeffer, How Should We Then Live? The rise and decline of western thought and culture, (Old Tappan, N.J.: Fleming H. Revel Co., 1976), 14-117.

good but still need to improve. To them, ignorance is the problem, and education is the solution. They also believe humans are free and independently responsible for themselves—even though they often try to speed the process of improvement by government intervention, which typically results in less freedom. Humanists hope that if we all become educated, we will make better choices and eliminate crime, poverty, and war.

The lie is not that the human race can improve. The lie is that education is sufficient alone to solve our problems. The assumption that we are essentially good people feels good, but it ignores the reality of our sinful nature. It ignores that we are sinners in need of a Savior. But education alone does not make us God-like rulers. We need more than education; we need transformation (Romans 12:1-2).

Yes, education *is* necessary. As God-like rulers, we are called to subdue our environment to create order and fill it with meaning, purpose, and value. The universe is complex. Cultures are complex. People are complex. Education helps us be aware of and understand this complexity. Without education, we are ill-equipped to fulfill our purpose. I like the definition on my wife's coffee cup: "Teaching: The profession that makes all other professions possible." Education is necessary, but it is not sufficient.

Part of the humanistic lie is that we are sufficient. Through self improvement, we can become who we need to be to solve our problems. We can be the solution! This lie is especially tempting to men. We love to be the white knight, the superhero, the one upon whom others admire and depend. Ultimately, trying to solve the world's problems on our own only leads to burnout. We were not created to be saviors of the world. God-like rulers humbly recognize their limitations and trust in God's unlimited ability and desire to be their solution.

King Adam Before and After His Fall

Pastor Hank needs to appreciate that God has not called him to a life of burnout and strained family relationships. By faith, he could let God be God over the ministry of the church. It is not Hank's ministry or his church, but God's kingdom, God's ministry, and God's church. If a program is genuinely needed, God will supply the resources and people to lead it in His time.

Hank can bring much more order and fullness to his flock's spiritual emptiness by praying for sensitivity to how and where God is working. Then by equipping his congregation to use their spiritual gifts to speak the truth in love to one another and their community (Ephesians 4:1-16), he could restore the original design of God's institution, the church. Then Hank would be released from needing to do many ministries not aligned with his spiritual gifts. Instead, by using his extra time to fill his family relationships with meaning, purpose, and value, Hank could not only receive the blessings of a healthy support system but also model to his congregation how to strengthen God's institution, the family.

Fantasies and Realms

Part of the original mandate was to "fill the earth and subdue it" (Gen 1:28). The phrase "and subdue it" strongly suggests that ruling over the environment means that we produce meaningful change outside of ourselves. Today's fallen God-like rulers lack fulfillment when they fail to subdue, but instead seek fulfillment in fantasies rather than "realms."

When we think about fantasy, our thoughts often turn to that particular form of entertainment, whether in books, film, or video games. In response to the Harry Potter series, Gene Veith noted that fantasy literature has "always been a staple of children's entertainment." He pointed out that,

The problem is not with fantasy, which is simply an exercise of the imagination. A work of fantasy can shape the imagination of its audience in either harmful or helpful ways. The challenge is to discern the difference between good fantasy and bad fantasy, recognizing not only its content but also its effects on the reader.[48]

Beyond just a form of entertainment, fantasy can also be a thought experiment, the opportunity to explore the possible implications of a "what if" actually becoming a reality. By removing the constraints of current reality, our imagination can explore possibilities hidden to us. One problem solving strategy is to conceive an impossible solution to an unsolvable problem. In other words, finding a solution that will fully satisfy the need, or solve the problem, even if implementing the plan, appears to be impossible. The next step is merely finding a way to make the impossible possible. This is how a fantasy can become fruitful.

I currently teach at a school about 100 miles from Wichita, Kansas. I ask my students if they thought it would be possible for me to get to Wichita in 30 minutes. The typical response is, "No way! That would be impossible." Then I ask them, "What if I was being life-flighted to Wichita because it was a matter of life or death? Or, what if I arranged for a private charter on a plane? Or, what if I invented my own "Jetson" style flying car?" The point is that an impossible solution might one day become possible if I can marshal the resources to make a fruitful fantasy a reality.

Imagination is a God given gift that is essential to the process of God-like ruling. Steven Covey explained, that everything is created

---

48 Gene Edward Veith (April 20, 2009), "Good Fantasy and Bad Fantasy," Accessed on 9/4/20 from: https://www.equip.org/article/good-fantasy-and-bad-fantasy/

twice.[49] We first create in our minds, then in the physical world. In this sense, fantasy is just the first step toward transforming ourselves and our world.

The problem begins when fantasies become an end in themselves. Rather than serving as a bridge to a new reality, a fantasy can become a quick and easy, but insufficient, substitute for what will satisfy the need. A sterile fantasy, one that only distracts us from producing a new reality, is like eating cotton candy. It is initially sweet but leaves us hungry and unfulfilled. When a thought experiment of our imagination leads us to a dead-end, God-like rulers reject the sterile fantasy and explore other possible solutions. In faith, they never give up on the possibility of a new reality aligned with the purposes and plans of God.

Realms, on the other hand, are the goal of fertile fantasies and the result of God-like ruling. Your realms are your circles of godly influence. Jesus must be the king over the realms that you have been entrusted with, or else they are sterile fantasies. James 4:2-3 states, "You do not have because you do not ask God. When you ask, you do not receive, because you ask with wrong motives, that you may spend what you get on your pleasures." The author is writing about people who first attempt to get what they want on their own without seeking God's answer to their needs. When they finally ask God, their concern is all about what they want, instead of what God wants in their situation.

Fallen God-like rulers, including myself, often listen to the lie that they are responsible for meeting the needs that, in reality, only God can fulfill. Our journey to becoming restored God-like rulers is long and often filled with self-induced pain caused by listening to this lie. When we try to fill those needs ourselves, we inevitably fail. And when we fail enough times, we can eventually give up hope in a new personal reality,

---

49 Steven Covey, The Seven Habits of Highly Effective People, Powerful lessons in personal change, (New York: Simon and Schuster, 2004), 106.

and settle for a faithless fantasy that leaves us empty and broken. The ultimate solution is to give up faith in ourselves and our resources and finally return home to the Father. He is ever watching for the prodigal to leave a life of fantasy and come home to reality.

In summary, we did find evidence that Adam was separating and filling his environment before his fall into rebellion. His separation of himself from the other animals, his naming of Eve, and his responsibility to work and care for the garden confirm that Adam's ruling was to use the same processes God used in creation. However, because of the sin of Adam's race, the concept of ruling changed as humans believed the lies of the enemy, and so, we became worthless for the purpose of glorifying God. Our capacity to rule was marred but not destroyed by our rebellion. Therefore, we find broken God-like rulers in modern society who are unfulfilled because they have rejected ruling over their environment within the Kingdom of God as God-like rulers for the glory of God. Only through the transforming power of the Spirit can we relearn how to rule as God intended us to.

King Adam Before and After His Fall

Discussion Questions

1. What are some changes you have observed in your culture that indicate a downward spiral away from God's order and will?

2. In what contexts are you tempted to take control instead of letting God be God over the situation?

3. What activities do you do that help you the most to transform to be more like Jesus?

4. What sterile fantasies are most tempting to you?

5. What fertile fantasies inspire you the most?

5

How God Rules the Fallen God-like Rulers

Fallen God-like rulers need to be restored. Until they find their way back to God through Jesus Christ, they are separated from the God who loves them. This separation causes them to live an empty way of life (1 Peter 1:18) that leaves them unfulfilled. The "radah" hypothesis is that since God used the processes of separating and filling to rule over His creation, He designed Adam to separate and fill his environment in order to be the God-likeness on earth. The first test of this hypothesis was to explore what we know about Adam's activity prior to the fall to see if he was ruling his realm like God ruled all He created. The second test of the "radah" hypothesis will be to explore how God rules over the fallen God-like rulers. Does God rule over our brokenness in a different way, or does He use the same processes of separating and filling to restore us?

The God Who is Separate and Full

This second test of the "radah" hypothesis begins with the sin that led God to separate Himself from Adam and Eve. Some who are only vaguely aware of the story assume that Adam's sin was having sex with Eve. On the contrary, Adam's sin was rebelling against the separation between God and himself. Adam believed the serpent's lie that by eating the fruit from the tree of the knowledge of good and evil, he would become more like God.

Ever since the Enlightenment, our culture has placed the supreme value on knowledge. Knowledge is power. Knowledge enables us to make wise choices. What could be wrong with Adam gaining more knowledge? We assume that gaining knowledge is always good and avoiding knowledge is always bad, but not so in this case. God had set a boundary between himself and Adam; the knowledge of good and evil. Instead of Adam appreciating his separateness from the animals by having a spirit to communicate with God, Adam sought to invade the boundary between himself and God. Believing Satan's lie, Adam attempted to use the one thing God had forbidden to try to "unseparate" himself from God.

Adam's attempt to be God was an attack on the very nature of God. Of all the attributes ascribed to God, only one attribute is revealed to be continually announced in heaven:

> Each of the four living creatures had six wings and was covered with eyes all around, even under its wings. Day and night they never stop saying: "'Holy, holy, holy is the Lord God Almighty,' who was, and is, and is to come." (Revelation 4:8)

In the Old Testament, the Hebrew word translated "holy" is "qadosh" and it means "to be separate." God is separate from everything and everyone. This separateness makes God absolutely unique; there is no one like Him. The opposite of "qadosh" is "khol" which means "common or profane."[50] To make something or someone "holy" or "sacred" means to separate them for a special purpose. For instance, if

---

50 Thomas McComiskey, "Qadash," in R. Laird Harris, Gleason Archer, and Bruce Waltke, eds., Theological Wordbook of the Old Testament, (Chicago: Moody Press, 1980), 2:786-789.

How God Rules the Fallen God-like Rulers

I were to set aside money to pay my rent, I could say that this money is "sacred" by being separated from the rest of the money that was not designated for any particular purpose. If I were to combine the rent money with the rest to make some purchase, I would be violating the "sacredness" or "holiness" of the rent money.

But God is not just holy; He is "holy, holy, holy." In Hebrew, a word is repeated for emphasis, but if repeated a third time, it expresses the superlative.[51] God is the most separate of all!

To be separated means more than being different or being in a different location. If this were the limit of what it means to be separate, then God would not be entirely separate. First, because when He created us in His image, we were originally not completely separate from God. Adam was designed to resemble God, to be an image of God. Second, He is not separate as in being far away. As Apostle Paul told the Athenians, "For in Him we live and move and have our being" (Acts 17:28).

Beyond being different or in a different location, being separated in this context perhaps more significantly means being ordered. Ordered separateness is not random, as the result of a bomb blast. Instead, this type of separation creates meaningful categories, and meaningful categories are the basis of order. God is "holy, holy, holy" because he is perfectly ordered. The Trinity is ordered by having three distinct persons. Each person in the Trinity has His own personality and function, which creates three meaningful categories within the God-head: the Father, Son, and Holy Spirit. If God were not completely ordered, whatever He created would reflect the same level of

---

51 Alan Johnson, "Revelation." in Frank Gaebelein, J.D.Douglas, James Montgomery Boice, and Merrill Tenney, eds., The Expositor's Bible Commentary, (Grand Rapids: Zondervan Publishing House, 1981), 12:463.

chaos He possessed. But at the end of creation week, God surveyed all that He had made and declared it to be "very good" (Gen 1:31).

The next question concerns the fulness of God. The Greek word in the New Testament commonly translated "fulness" is "plaeroma," and as a term of measurement conveys the meaning of completeness, or "the whole," as in "the full measure."[52] This word is a synonym of "telios" generally translated "perfect" or "complete." If God were not full, He Himself would not be perfect. Nor could God fill others if His fulness was not more than just complete but also overflowing. In the prologue of his gospel, John wrote, "Out of His fulness we have all received grace in place of grace already given." Merrill Tenney explained that the meaning of the Greek idiom is that "When one supply of grace is exhausted, another is available.[53] The word picture is like the manna fresh each morning; there is new grace for each day.[54]

With this abundant and overflowing grace, the Father fills the Son so that the Son might fill all of creation. Colossians 1:19 reveals that God was pleased to have all His fullness dwell in Him (Christ). He did this so that Christ could fill us so that we, the Body of Christ, might be "the fullness of Him who fills everything in every way." (Ephesians 1:23)

Remember, in the "radah" hypothesis, filling means to ascribe to someone meaning, purpose, and value. God the Father filled God the Son by ascribing to Jesus the meaning of being the "the Lamb of God,

---

52 Delling, G. (1968). Plaeroma. The Theological Dictionary of the New Testament. Kittle, G. and Friedrich, G. (Eds.), Bromiley, G.W. (Trans.). Grand Rapids, MI: W.B. Eerdmans Publishing Co.

53 Merrill Tenney, "The Gospel of John," in Frank Gaebelein, J.D.Douglas, James Montgomery Boice, and Merrill Tenney, eds., The Expositor's Bible Commentary, (Grand Rapids, MI: Zondervan Publishing House, 1981), 9:33.

54 A.T. Robertson, "The Fourth Gospel," in Word Pictures in the New Testament, (Nashville, TN: Broadman Press, 1932), 5:16.

who takes away the sin of the world!" (John 1:29) He filled the Son with purpose by sending Jesus to be born in a manger, to be tempted as we are, and ultimately suffer death on the cross for our sins. (Ephesians 3:10-11, Hebrews 4:15, Philippians 2:6-8) Finally, because of Jesus's submission to the Father, the Father filled the Son by ascribing to Jesus the greatest value of all. Philippians 2:9-11 reveals:

> [9] Therefore God exalted him to the highest place
> and gave him the name that is above every name,
> [10] that at the name of Jesus every knee should bow,
> in heaven and on earth and under the earth,
> [11] and every tongue acknowledge that Jesus Christ is Lord,
> to the glory of God the Father.

God is perfectly separate from all of Creation so that He is perfectly ordered within Himself. The order of God, His absolute truth, provides us an anchor when we are cast adrift in the chaos of our brokenness. Because of His grace, God is overflowing with meaning, purpose, and value so that He might fill us, and we might in turn fill others. How blessed we are to have a God who is both holy, holy, holy, and overflowing with grace to us.

The God Who Separates

The next question is to what extent does God use separating and filling in the redemption of Adam's race. Adam's attempt to "unseparate" himself from God actually accomplished the opposite. Driven from the garden, Adam and Eve lost the fellowship of God and found they were even more separate from Him because God had separated Himself from their sin.

For the moment, let's focus on how God used separation to accomplish our salvation. Although there are many examples in the long story of our salvation, consider some of the more obvious:

Kings and Queens in the Kingdom of God

1. Adam and Eve are both separated from the fellowship of God (Gen 3:22-23)
2. Noah and his family are separated in the ark from God's judgment of the world (Gen 6-7)
3. Abram is separated from his homeland and heritage (Gen 12), then separated from the nations through the separation of his foreskin (Gen 17:1-14)
4. Ishmael, child of the handmaiden, is separated from Isaac, the child of promise (Gen 21:8-13)
5. Jacob and Esau are separated into different nations (Gen 25:23)
6. Joseph is separated from his family (Gen 37), then from prison to reign over Egypt (Gen 41)
7. Moses is separated from his people to be raised in Pharaoh's court (Exodus 2:1-10), then separated from Egypt to the desert (Exodus 2:11-22), then separated from shepherding to lead his people (Exodus 3), and finally is used to separate the Israelites out of Egypt (Exodus 12-14)
8. The Israelites are separated from the nations by the law to be God's people (Leviticus 15:31)
9. The Jews are separated from the promised land and exiled to Babylon (2 Kings 24:10-14) to separate them from idolatry (2 Kings 22:17)
10. God separates Himself from His only Son as judgment for our sins (Matthew 27:45-46)
11. God separates the elect out of the kingdom of darkness and into His glorious light (Ephesians 5:8)
12. God separates our sins from us as far as the east is from the west. (Psalm 103:12)
13. God separates believers for different ministries by giving

How God Rules the Fallen God-like Rulers

    spiritual gifts (Romans 12:6-8, 1 Corinthians 12-14, 1 Peter 4:10-11)

14. Finally, God's judgment will, in the end, separate the righteous from the unrighteous. (Matthew 13:49)

Throughout the story of our salvation, God has repeatedly used separation as a means to accomplish it. Not only this, but God repeatedly calls us to separate ourselves from the beliefs and customs of this world:

> Do not conform to the pattern of this world, but be transformed by the renewing of your mind. Then you will be able to test and approve what God's will is—his good, pleasing, and perfect will. (Romans 12:2)

> What agreement is there between the temple of God and idols? For we are the temple of the living God. As God has said: "I will live with them and walk among them, and I will be their God, and they will be my people." Therefore, "Come out from them and be separate, says the Lord. Touch no unclean thing, and I will receive you." (2 Corinthians 6:16-17)

> You adulterous people, don't you know that friendship with the world means enmity against God? Therefore, anyone who chooses to be a friend of the world becomes an enemy of God. (James 4:4)

> Do not love the world or anything in the world. If anyone loves the world, love for the Father is not in them. For everything in the world: the lust of the flesh, the lust of the eyes,

and the pride of life—comes not from the Father but from the world. (1 John 2:15-16)

We "were redeemed from the empty way of life handed down to us from our ancestors" (1 Peter 1:18) by being called out from them, and to be separate (i.e., different and ordered) "so that the grace that is reaching more and more people may cause thanksgiving to overflow to the glory of God (2 Corinthians 4:15). In other words, we have been called out of a life that leaves us empty to be fulfilled by letting the testimony of our new lives attract more people to receive God's grace which ultimately brings more glory to God.

The God Who Fills

Separating is the initial process God uses to redeem us, but the ultimate goal is to fill us with meaning, purpose, and value. In other words, to return us to Adam's state before the fall when he had meaning (the God-like ruler on earth), purpose (to glorify God by ruling over his environment), and value (proclaimed with the rest of creation to be "very good"). When something is full, God calls it good. In this sense, fullness is a synonym for goodness. The relationship between fullness and goodness is evident throughout the Scriptures. Consider the following brief list of examples:

1. The Promised Land was described as flowing (over full) with milk and honey (Exodus 3:8)
2. The blessings of God included a full life (Exodus 23:25-26)
3. Joseph's children were blessed with the best gifts of the earth and its fullness (Deuteronomy 33:16)
4. The earth is the Lord's and all the fullness thereof (Psalm 24:1)

How God Rules the Fallen God-like Rulers

5. Paul's prayer for the Ephesians was that they might be filled to the measure of all the fullness of God (Ephesians 3:19)
6. The goal of spiritual growth is described as attaining to the whole measure of the fullness of Christ (Ephesians 4:13)
7. Paul urges the Ephesians to be filled with the Spirit (literally: constantly being kept filled) Ephesians 5:18
8. God was pleased to have all his fullness dwell in Christ (Colossians 1:19)
9. Believers have been given fullness in Christ (Colossians 2:10)

The opposite is also true. Emptiness is equated with worthlessness and disgrace:

1. Naomi laments that God had brought her back from Moab empty (Ruth 1:21)
2. God does not listen to empty pleas (Job 35:13)
3. God's word does not return to him empty (Isaiah 55:11)
4. Rebellious Israel was described as an empty vine (Hosea 10:1)

In the story of redemption, we find that creation is corrupted by those who leave their ordered state to venture outside their purpose. Both Lucifer's and Adam's attempts to be like God were rebellions against God's established order. Sin also turned the fullness that God had created into:

1. Emptiness (1 Peter 1:18: you were redeemed from the empty way of life handed down to you from your ancestors),
2. Meaninglessness (Ecclesiastes 1:2: "Meaningless! Meaningless!" says the Teacher. "Utterly meaningless! Everything is meaningless.")

3. Worthlessness (Romans 3:12: All have turned away; they have together become worthless; there is no one who does good, not even one")

Through the process of redemption, God transforms us from emptiness, meaninglessness, and worthlessness to restore us to our original purpose for the praise of His glory. He truly makes all things beautiful. Does God ascribe meaning, purpose, and value to the redeemed?

Remember, the concept of meaning is defined in two ways, first, as a spatial relationship between two people or things in which either the physical or emotional distance can be described,[55] and second, as a functional relationship in which one element instrumentally affects change in the other's behavior.[56] Think of a functional relationship as a change in one thing that causes a change in something else.

Both the spatial and functional definitions of meaning are applicable to the process of redemption. First, significant to Paul's theology of redemption is that the redeemed are now "in Christ." This is a favorite phrase of Apostle Paul. Here are some examples:

> For we know that since Christ was raised from the dead, he cannot die again; death no longer has mastery over him. The death he died, he died to sin once for all; but the life he lives, he lives to God. In the same way, count yourselves dead to sin but alive to God in Christ Jesus (Romans 6:9-11).

> Therefore, there is now no condemnation for those who are in Christ Jesus, because through Christ Jesus, the law of the Spirit

---

[55] Fauconnier, G. (1997). Mappings in Thought and Language. Cambridge, England: Cambridge University Press.
[56] Daniel Dennett, Brainstorms, Philosophical Essays on Mind and Psychology, (Cambridge, MA: The MIT Press, 1978), 80.

who gives life has set you free from the law of sin and death. (Romans 8:1-2)

God chose the lowly things of this world and the despised things—and the things that are not—to nullify the things that are, so that no one may boast before him. It is because of him that you are in Christ Jesus, who has become for us wisdom from God—that is, our righteousness, holiness and redemption. (1 Corinthians 1:28-30)

Praise be to the God and Father of our Lord Jesus Christ, who has blessed us in the heavenly realms with every spiritual blessing in Christ. For he chose us in him before the creation of the world to be holy and blameless in his sight. (Ephesians 1:3-4)

The concept of being "in Christ" is at the core of the Evangelical understanding of the gospel. James D. G. Dunn noted that the believer in Christ is,

> "baptized in the Spirit into Christ (Rom. 6:3; 1 Cor. 12:13; 2 Cor. 1:21; Gal. 3:27); he has died with Christ, is crucified with Christ, his life is hid with Christ in God etc. (Rom. 6:3 f., 8; 8:17; Gal. 2:19 f.; Eph. 2:5; Phil. 1:23; Col. 2:20; 3:1, 3; I Thess. 5:10); his present life in all its aspects is lived in Christ (e.g., Rom. 6:11; 8:39; 1 Cor. 15:22; 2 Cor. 5:17, 19; Gal. 24; Phil. 2:1; Col. 1:28; I Thess. 2:14); he is a member of the body of Christ (Rom. 12:5; 1 Cor. 12:12, 2'7 etc.); Christ is the offspring of Abraham to whom the promise has been made, and all who identify themselves with Christ are counted as Abraham's children (Gal. 3:16, 26-9)."[57]

---

57 James D.G. Dunn, "Paul's Understanding of the Death of Jesus,"

Kings and Queens in the Kingdom of God

Those who are "in Christ" are ascribed meaning by the Father based on their relationship to Christ. We are saved, not by our own righteousness, but rather by being seen by God as "in Christ," and through this spatial relationship, we have His righteousness credited to our account.

Second, the meaning ascribed to the redeemed by God could also be described as functional. We are the workmanship of Christ (Ephesians 2:10) in the sense that through the power of the Holy Spirit, our behavior is being transformed from the acts of the sinful nature to the fruits of the Spirit (Galatians 5:16-25). Additionally, every believer receives a spiritual gift (1 Peter 4:10-11) which defines their function within the Body of Christ (Romans 12:6-8, I Corinthians 12-14, Ephesians 4:11-13). Therefore, the redeemed are meaningful to God because His word is producing change in our lives and also because He has gifted each of us with spiritual gifts to effect change in others.

Ephesians 1:11 reveals the purpose ascribed to the redeemed:

> "In him we were also chosen, having been predestined according to the plan of him who works out everything in conformity with the purpose of his will in order that we, who were the first to hope in Christ, might be for the praise of his glory."

Paul repeats these themes in Ephesians 2:7, "in order that in the coming ages he might show the incomparable riches of his grace, expressed in his kindness to us in Christ Jesus."

Believers are not redeemed out of bondage into anything in particular. God had a design, a plan for the church—that her redemption might glorify (i.e., magnify) a previously unrevealed characteristic of God: His grace. A similar purpose for the redeemed is to reveal God's

---

Robert Banks, ed., Reconciliation and Hope. New Testament Essays on Atonement and Eschatology Presented to L.L. Morris on his 60th Birthday. (Carlisle: The Paternoster Press, 1974), 125-141.

How God Rules the Fallen God-like Rulers

mercy: "What if He did this (i.e., called us to Himself) to make the riches of His glory known to the objects of His mercy, whom He prepared in advance for glory" (Romans 9:22-23). Beyond these general purposes, each individual believer receives a special purpose in God's plan (1 Corinthians 2:9, Ephesians 2:10; 4:16).

Finally, does God ascribe value to the redeemed? Remember, apart from God, we became "worthless" (Romans 3:12). The answer lies in the value of the item God was willing to exchange to redeem us. How valuable was the Son of God, whose blood was shed to purchase our redemption? It is not that we deserved His redemption, but Jesus knew He had the ability to transform the worthless ones into the "joy set before him" (Hebrews 12:2). Perhaps the depth of God's esteem for our potential value is the greatest challenge of our faith. Consider that no detail of our lives escapes His attention (Matthew 10:28-30), and yet He has promised to never leave us (Matthew 28:20, Hebrews 13:5). We are the apple of His eye (Zechariah 3:8), His delight (Deuteronomy 30:9, Zephaniah 3:17), and His joy (John 15:9-11). The greatest demonstration of God's love for us is that while we were still in rebellion against all that He had designed for us, He sacrificed His only Son for our sins (Ephesians 2:1-5). God foresaw our great potential value that would be revealed when we would be transformed into God-like rulers.

That is who God saw that we could become, but our rebellion has created chaos and emptiness that God would not accept. The intense resolve of God to restore His rule over creation is revealed in the immense power He exerts to restore us,

> That power is like the working of his mighty strength, which he exerted in Christ when he raised him from the dead and seated him at his right hand in the heavenly realms, far above all rule and authority, power and dominion, and every title that

can be given, not only in the present age but also in the one to come. And God placed all things under his feet and appointed him to be head over everything for the church, which is his body, the fullness of him who fills everything in every way. (Ephesians 1:19-23)

God clearly forced His will upon the rebellion and separated Christ from the rest of creation. God did this by ascribing to Christ meaning (ruler overall), purpose (headship over the church), and therefore value (seated at His right hand). The meaning, purpose, and value of Christ are also emphasized in Colossians 1:15-20,

1. Meaning: The Son is the image of the invisible God, the firstborn over all creation.
2. Purpose: For in Him all things were created: things in heaven and on earth, visible and invisible, whether thrones or powers or rulers or authorities; all things have been created through Him and for Him. He is before all things, and in Him all things hold together. And He is the head of the body, the church; He is the beginning and the firstborn from among the dead, so that in everything He might have the supremacy.
3. Value: For God was pleased to have all His fullness dwell in Him, and through Him to reconcile to Himself all things, whether things on earth or things in heaven, by making peace through His blood, shed on the cross.

Note that the process begins with the exertion of God's will to re-establish His order and is completed by His filling everything in every way. The beauty of God's love is that He fills us with Himself. He comes to live in us and fills us with meaning and purpose to restore our value. This is how God rules the fallen God-like rulers.

The Destiny of the Sons of Adam and Daughters of Eve

Through God's redemption, we have a destiny beyond our ability to comprehend:

> "What no eye has seen, what no ear has heard, and what no human mind has conceived"—the things God has prepared for those who love him—these are the things God has revealed to us by his Spirit. (1 Corinthians 2:9-10)

God has promised that our current struggle to reign over our sinful nature will one day be over. Sin will no longer have power over us, nor will we forever reap the penalty of sin in the decay and death of our bodies. Apostle Paul explains in Romans 8:18-23,

> I consider that our present sufferings are not worth comparing with the glory that will be revealed in us. For the creation waits in eager expectation for the children of God to be revealed. For the creation was subjected to frustration, not by its own choice, but by the will of the one who subjected it, in hope that the creation itself will be liberated from its bondage to decay and brought into the freedom and glory of the children of God. We know that the whole creation has been groaning as in the pains of childbirth right up to the present time. Not only so, but we ourselves, who have the first fruits of the Spirit, groan inwardly as we wait eagerly for our adoption to sonship, the redemption of our bodies.

Not only will we receive new bodies that will live forever, but we will also be joined in marriage to Christ. Scripture calls the church "the Bride of Christ," and after the final spiritual battle, we will celebrate at the Marriage Feast of the Lamb. Revelation 19:6-9 reveals,

> Then I heard what sounded like a great multitude, like the roar of rushing waters and like loud peals of thunder, shouting: "Hallelujah! For our Lord God Almighty reigns. Let us rejoice

> and be glad and give him glory! For the wedding of the Lamb has come, and his bride has made herself ready. Fine linen, bright and clean, was given her to wear." (Fine linen stands for the righteous acts of God's holy people.) Then the angel said to me, "Write this: Blessed are those who are invited to the wedding supper of the Lamb!" And he added, "These are the true words of God."

Never again will we be separated from the fellowship of God. Never again will we sense an emptiness in our soul. We will forever be completely filled with His love. During the millennium, those who resisted the mark of the beast will reign with Christ. Apostle John writes in Revelation 20:4,

> I saw thrones on which were seated those who had been given authority to judge. And I saw the souls of those who had been beheaded because of their testimony about Jesus and because of the word of God. They had not worshiped the beast or its image and had not received its mark on their foreheads or their hands. They came to life and reigned with Christ a thousand years.

Note that earlier in this chapter (20:15-16) we learn that after His victory over the rebellion, Christ will rule over the nations with an iron scepter. I interpret this as Christ will subdue the nations by force to bring His kingdom to earth. Then, after Satan is thrown into the Abyss, those who were beheaded by the antichrist come to life and reign with Christ for a thousand years. This however, does not necessarily mean that they will also be reigning over the nations. Christ can handle that by Himself. It is very conceivable that we will be restoring order and filling the earth with meaning purpose, and value.

How God Rules the Fallen God-like Rulers

But wait, there is more! Once God has re-established Eden and created a new heaven and a new earth, our ultimate destiny will be to reign with Christ forever:

> Then the angel showed me the river of the water of life, as clear as crystal, flowing from the throne of God and of the Lamb down the middle of the great street of the city. On each side of the river stood the tree of life, bearing twelve crops of fruit, yielding its fruit every month. And the leaves of the tree are for the healing of the nations. No longer will there be any curse. The throne of God and of the Lamb will be in the city, and his servants will serve him. They will see his face, and his name will be on their foreheads. There will be no more night. They will not need the light of a lamp or the light of the sun, for the Lord God will give them light. And they will reign forever and ever. (Revelation 22:1-5)

Please note again that at this point in the story, all those who rejected God have already been cast into the lake of fire. If we who believe will all reign forever and ever, what are we going to be ruling over? Certainly not each other! Instead, in this restored Eden, we will return to our original purpose of ruling over our environment: separating to create order and filling it with meaning, purpose, and value.

The story of Adam before he sinned, our salvation, and our ultimate destiny shows that we were designed to rule, redeemed to rule, and destined to rule. The key to connecting the end with the beginning is to see that we were created to glorify God by imitating how God rules: through separating and filling. Perhaps one reason our universe is infinite is so that we will never run out of opportunities to separate and fill for the glory of God!

Kings and Queens in the Kingdom of God

The next chapter will explore the effect of sin on the way that we rule. How has our sin distorted the way we rule? Is there evidence across a variety of cultures that humans tend to naturally separate and fill their environment? It's not pretty, but it is pretty amazing.

Discussion Questions

1. What are some people, places, or things that God has separated you from in the process of your salvation and growth in Christ?

2. How has God filled your emptiness with meaning, purpose, and value?

3. To what purpose has God called you?

4. What does ruling in eternity look like to you?

6

Jesus, Our Model Ruler

If Jesus came to show us how to live, in other words, to be the "Second Adam" (Romans 5:12-19); if ruling as God intended includes separating to create order and filling with meaning, purpose, and value, then we should see Jesus modeling these principles in His human life and ministry. Perhaps, before surveying the Gospels for specific examples of separating or filling, it would be helpful to explore one situation where all of the aspects of God-like ruling are present.

The Feeding of the Five Thousand

The story of the feeding the five thousand appears in all four gospels (Matthew 14, Mark 6, Luke 9, and John 6). As the story goes, Jesus had just received His twelve disciples back from their first experience at preaching repentance, driving out demons, and healing the sick. He had separated Himself from them so they could gain experience in what He had purposed for them to do after He had ascended. Realizing the exhausting effect of this kind of ministry, Jesus planned to separate them from the crowds to a remote place to fill them with rest.

However, when they landed their boat on the other side of the sea of Galilee, Jesus found that the crowds had followed Him and were waiting for Him there. Jesus "had compassion on them, because they were like sheep without a shepherd. So He began teaching them many things" (Mark 6:34). By teaching them, He did what a shepherd does: He fed His sheep. But He was not filling them with food yet. He was filling them with meaning by giving them greater understanding of the Kingdom of God. And perhaps more significantly, He was filling them with spatial meaning as people whom He, the Son of God, cared about deeply.

As the shadows grew long, the disciples wanted to separate themselves from the crowds. Jesus, however, saw an opportunity to fill His disciples with functional meaning. The disciples' plan was to send the people away hungry (i.e., empty), but Jesus insisted that they feed the crowd of 5,000 men and additional women and children. This led the disciples to question Jesus out of their lack of faith (i.e., their emptiness). Jesus then challenged them to take inventory, a type of order produced by separating those who had food with them from those who didn't. The passage read, "'How many loaves do you have?' he asked. 'Go and see.'"

When they returned with the little boy who had five loaves and two fish (probably more like five biscuits and two small fish), He asked them to give him the food. Jesus realized that if He started handing out free food to 5,000 plus hungry people, He would create pandemonium! Instead, He instructed the disciples to have the crown sit on the grass in groups of hundreds and fifties. By separating the crowd into smaller units, the order made them easier to serve, and by having them sit down, Jesus filled them with an expectation of receiving something.

"Taking the five loaves and the two fish and looking up to heaven, he gave thanks and broke the loaves. Then he gave them to his disciples to distribute to the people. He also divided the two fish among them all" (Mark 6:41). By giving thanks to the Father, Jesus was filling these loaves and fish with the meaning that they had been provided by God. Then He separated the food into twelve different baskets to be distributed by the twelve disciples. Where did the baskets come from? The same source as the food, I suppose: God provided! And after all the people ate and were satisfied, the twelve baskets that started with just a partial biscuit and a bit of fish wound up being filled with leftovers!

After the people saw the sign Jesus performed, they began to say, "Surely this is the Prophet who is to come into the world" (John 6:14). In other words, the people assigned meaning to the miracle. They were both right and wrong. He was the Messiah, but not with the goal they had in mind. Jesus wanted to save them from more than just the Romans, but to do that, He first had to save them from their sins. "Jesus, knowing that they intended to come and make him king by force, withdrew again to a mountain by himself" (John 6:15). So to fulfill His mission, just as He had to separate himself from the religious leaders, now He had to also separate Himself from those who wanted to make Him simply an earthly king.

From this event, we can see Jesus using the strategies of physically separating the people into groups to create order to physically fill the people with food. Beyond this, earlier by leaving the crowds of those who happened to be present and providing an opportunity for those who would be willing to walk several miles to hear Him teach, He separated out a special group of people to fill with meaning. However, the filling with purpose and value was yet to come because the people did not yet understand the fulness of His mission. Therefore He had to separate Himself from these people until the fulness of His time.

Ruling over His Realm

As mentioned in chapter four, one of the things that rulers do is establish their realms, their place of godly influence. To do this, they must identify and submit to the realm given them by God. Jesus' realm at the time of His earthly ministry was to "testify to the Truth" (John18:37) and "that whoever believes in him shall not perish but have eternal life" (John 3:16). To establish this realm (i.e., to stay on track with His mission), Jesus often had to separate Himself from the desires of others, telling them "It's not yet my time" or, "my time is near" (John 2:4, 7:6-8, 16:25; Matthew 26:18). At other times Jesus had to prioritize whom He would heal because He was "sent to the lost sheep of Israel" (Matthew 10:6, 15:24). Especially when His compassion overcame His initial plan, He was forced to leave His location in order to have the time to teach His disciples. Several times we find Jesus saying to His disciples, "Let's Go," or it is reported "He withdrew" or "He left there" (Mark 1:38; Matt. 4:12, 12:15, 14:13). Essentially, Jesus was intentional about filling His disciples with meaning, purpose, and value, and for that He needed time with them alone.

Separating Himself to the Father

Jesus kept His mission on track by separating Himself from even the disciples to listen to the Father (Mark 1:35, Luke 5:16, John 17:1). We learn in Luke 5:16 that "Jesus often withdrew to lonely places and prayed." We gained insight into this relationship when Jesus told the religious leaders,

> "Very truly I tell you, the Son can do nothing by himself; he can do only what he sees his Father doing, because whatever the Father does the Son also does. For the Father loves the Son and shows him all he does." (John 5:19-20)

Jesus followed the Father step by step. We don't know how much Jesus knew about everything He would do, but we find that Jesus was confident He was fulfilling His mission because "whatever the Father does the Son also does."

Finally, when opportunities arose, His custom was to teach the people (Mark 10:1, Luke 4:16). In other words, since His mission was to testify to the Truth that whosoever might believe, the gospel writers noted that Jesus was always teaching. He was filling us with the Truth by His teaching, both in word and deed. And yet, to fill His followers, Jesus first had to be filled by the Father. Colossians 1:19-20 reveals to us,

> For God was pleased to have all his fullness dwell in him, and through him to reconcile to himself all things, whether things on earth or things in heaven, by making peace through his blood, shed on the cross.

Subduing Chaos

To subdue the chaos of the world He was born into (i.e., to restore God's order), Jesus had to provide a very different understanding of who God is and His desire for the people. The Sadducees, having accepted only the five books of Moses as scripture, rejected the idea of life after death (Matthew 22:23-32). They emptied the people of any hope of a better life to come. The Pharisees did much the same thing but in a different way. They canonized so many traditions as requirements of God they made being fully obedient to them all effectively impossible. Jesus' charge against the Sadducees was that they were ignorant of the scriptures and the power of God, but the Pharisees He called hypocrites. They "nullified" with their traditions the very law they claimed to teach (Mark 7:5-13). Thus Jesus separated Himself from the teachers of the law and their false doctrine. But more than this, by teaching on the true nature of the Kingdom of God, He filled the "lost children of Israel" with hope for the future.

Fulfilling the Law

As Jesus taught on the Kingdom, He also filled the ten commandments with greater meaning. He explained that God's intent in the law was to condemn not just the acts, such as murder or adultery, but the condition of the heart that led to those behaviors (Matthew 5:21-30). However, Jesus filled one of the ten with a new meaning altogether. Of the fourth command, to remember the sabbath and keep it holy, Jesus simply said that He was the Lord of the Sabbath. He later explained that the rest God wanted us to experience was more than rest from physical labor; He also wants us to receive rest for our souls (Matthew 11:28-29). By this, Jesus meant that He, and only He, could fulfill all the requirements of the law for us and provide the way for us to enter into God's rest, to rest from working for our salvation (Hebrews 4:1-11).

Ascribing Meaning

When Jesus called Peter, Andrew, James, and John to be His disciples, He said, "Come, follow me, and I will send you out to fish for people" (Matthew 4:19). Jesus' offer to these minimally educated fishermen was to receive two new meanings from Him. First, a new spatial meaning both in the physical sense (to be with Him) and in the emotional sense because following Him meant accepting the role of a trusted student and confidant. The disciples would be trusted with explanations that would be kept from others. Second, Jesus' offer was to receive a new functional meaning. Notice their calling was optional. They could refuse and some did (Luke 9:57-62). Jesus uses influence, not force, to rule over us. However, if they chose to follow Jesus, their purpose in God's Kingdom would be forever changed. But, to accomplish that purpose, they would need to become transformed to function as fishers of people rather than fishers of fish. Jesus now offers this new spatial and functional meaning to all of us.

Jesus also ascribed new meanings to the rich symbolism in the Levitical system of worship. In response to criticism that His disciples did not fast, Jesus used the analogy that people do not pour new wine into old wineskins. "If they do, the skins will burst; the wine will run out and the wineskins will be ruined. No, they pour new wine into new wineskins, and both are preserved" (Matthew 9:17). Jesus explained at the last supper that a new covenant between God and humans was being established which would require new forms of worship (i.e., in spirit and in truth) with new symbolism and meaning. The life, death, and resurrection of Jesus now has for us both new spatial meaning (being "in Christ" and the "Bride of Christ") and new functional meaning (The Body of Christ, "created in Christ Jesus to do good works, which God prepared in advance for us to do" Ephesians 2:10).

Creating Value

When the Sanhedrin "saw the courage of Peter and John and realized that they were unschooled, ordinary men, they were astonished and they took note that these men had been with Jesus" (Acts 4:13). This comment was made after Peter and John healed a lame man, and after being arrested, boldly testified to the Sanhedrin that He was healed in the name of Jesus Christ whom they had crucified. Just weeks before, this same John had assumed that if they ventured to Jerusalem they would all be killed and Peter denied even knowing Jesus three times. Jesus changes people. Of course, their bold testimony also occurred after the day of Pentecost when they were filled with the Holy Spirit. Once Peter and John were like all the other people, "worthless" (Romans 3:12) for bringing glory to God. Now they were able to both separate the lies of the Sanhedrin from the Truth and to "fill Jerusalem with their teaching" (Acts 5:28). By receiving from God new meaning (as disciples) and purpose (as apostles), they now had value for fulfilling God's purpose.

Peter and John had become God-like rulers, but they were still sinners by nature and continued to be transformed (Galatians 2:11-13). The next chapter will explore the effect of sin on the way that we rule. There is widely accepted empirical evidence across various cultures that humans continue to naturally separate and fill their environment. How has our sin distorted the way we rule? It's not pretty, but it is amazing.

Jesus, Our Model Ruler

Discussion Questions

1. What kinds of chaos in your life has Jesus subdued, helping you reflect God's order?

2. What does Jesus mean to you? What do you think you mean to Jesus?

Kings and Queens in the Kingdom of God

3. What is your primary functional meaning to the Kingdom of God?

4. How has Jesus added value to your life?

7

Hard-Wired to Separate

The "radah" hypothesis is that we are designed to separate and fill our environment with meaning, purpose, and value. Another test of this hypothesis would be to look for evidence that these processes come naturally to us. Have psychologists observed these processes when researching human behavior? Specifically, what widely accepted and verified observations of human biology and behavior provide evidence to support the "radah" hypothesis? None of the psychological research presented in this chapter is new. They have been in Psychology 101 textbooks for decades. What might be new is the integration of these psychological theories with a Biblical view of human nature.

In this chapter, our natural tendency to separate to create order will be explored. Chaos tends to frustrate us, and creating order tends to reduce that stress, sometimes even to the point of enjoyment. Many forms of entertainment simply provide a challenge to create order out of chaos. Jigsaw and crossword puzzles, and logic games like Sudoku are examples of how we get pleasure from separating to create order. However, depending upon our cognitive development, our personality, and several other factors that make each of us unique, various types of chaos affect us differently.

Designed to Create Order

Separating to create order is part of our DNA. Research has shown that immediately after birth, newborns prefer their mother's voice to all other voices. Even while in the womb, babies are separating the muffled sounds of the voice of their mother from the voices of other people. Some might point out that this preference for the mother is a learned behavior, that the baby is learning even before birth. However, this ability to learn depends upon the pre-born baby already having the ability to distinguish between sounds and form associations between them by the sixth month of gestation.[58] Ordering our experience through our sensations is pre-wired into our neural network.

Sensation

Sensation is the process of transforming the physical stimulation of our sensory organs into neural impulses that are delivered to the brain. Light enters our eyes, sound waves strike our eardrums, the molecules in our food stimulate our tastebuds and olfactory receptors in our nasal cavity, and through touch, the nerve endings in our skin gather data from the outside world.

A human optic nerve has almost 1 million ganglion fibers, each of which can send a separate bit of data to your brain. The auditory nerve contains about 30,000 fibers to help us distinguish between sounds. Humans have some 20 million olfactory receptors to enable us to separate between different smells.[59] Our skin has three different types of nerve endings: those that sense pressure, vibrations, and texture,

---

58 David Myers and Nathan Dewall, Exploring Psychology, 10th edition, (New York: Worth Publishers, 2016), 123.
59 Ibid, 199-242.

those that sense temperature, and others that deliver signals of pain.[60] Together, our God-given ability of sensation enables us to distinguish or separate information from the world around us.

Humans can differentiate between 10,000 different odors.[61] As an example, neuroscientist Stuart Firestein, who studies the sense of smell, found that the addition of only one carbon atom and two hydrogen atoms to a hexyl acetate molecule changes the smell produced by this molecule from a banana to a pear.[62] I find it amazing that our sense of smell can distinguish the difference between two completely different smells produced by only three atoms.

How sensitive is the human sense of touch? Researchers have discovered that we are sensitive enough to feel the difference between surfaces that differ by just a single layer of molecules. Humans can also readily separate between many everyday surfaces such as glass, metal, wood, and plastic. We can do this because these surfaces have different textures or draw heat away from the finger at different rates.[63]

Another example of our ability to differentiate between sensations is found in our sense of sight. The visible spectrum of colors our eyes are designed to sense is an extremely small portion of the continuum from very low energy (e.g., radio waves) to very high energy (e.g., gamma rays). Typically, the human eye can detect wavelengths from 380 to 700 nanometers. A nanometer is one-billionth of a meter or one-millionth of a millimeter. Violet has the shortest wavelength, at

---

60 Sense of Touch, accessed on 2/28/2021 from: https://learning-center.homesciencetools.com/article/skin-touch/
61 Accessed 3/7/21 from https://courses.lumenlearning.com/boundless-psychology/chapter/sensory-processes/
62 Accessed 3/7/21 from https://www.ted.com/talks/stuart_firestein_the_pursuit_of_ignorance#t-827095
63 Accessed 3/7/21 from https://ucsdnews.ucsd.edu/pressrelease/less_than_skin_deep_humans_can_feel_molecular_differences_between_nearly_id

around 380 nanometers, and red has the longest wavelength, at around 700 nanometers.[64]

The amazing design of our sense organs to distinguish very small differences in the light waves, sound waves, and molecules that find their way up our nose is strong evidence that we were designed to separate.

Automated Decisions to Separate and Fill

Many of our decisions are made unconsciously by the automated system in our minds. Maddalena Marini (2018) explains,

> The human mind is characterized by two systems that process information from the environment: the controlled and automatic systems. The controlled system can be defined as a "reflective" structure in which the processing of information is under the intentional and conscious control of the individual. The automatic system, instead, can be described as a "reflex" of the mind in which the processing of the information occurs outside of our awareness and consciousness.

When we stand up from our chair in the office to grab a book off shelf, we know automatically what to do to achieve a fully standing position. We do not think, "How should I move my body?" or "Where should I put my feet?" We automatically know the situation and the proper process to reach our goal based on our past experience.

DO NOT READ THIS MESSAGE

---

64 Accessed 3/7/21 from https://science.nasa.gov/ems/09_visiblelight

Did you read the message? Of course, you did! Reading single words and short phrases is an automatic process that requires no voluntary effort.[65] The ability to develop an automatic system is a capability with which we are born. The resulting system is based on prior experience, but the ability to connect those experiences and create automatic responses to distinguish sensations and fill with meaning comes from God's design of God-like rulers.

Grouping to Create Order

If we are pre-wired to distinguish between sensations, they must be then separated and assigned to groups for those sensations to represent a meaningful order. Groups are formed by establishing two things: group membership requirements and group boundaries. This sounds complicated, but it is a staple of a kindergarten curriculum. Many kindergarten teachers have helped their students develop this skill by having them sort buttons of different colors, shapes, or by the number of holes they have. In a simple example like this, the group membership characteristic (buttons with two holes) is the same as the group boundary (buttons that do not have two holes).

As life gets more complicated, membership and boundaries become complex and different from each other. Group membership might be "the person to whom I am legally married," but the boundaries are the rules or expectations (hopefully communicated) that one person has for another. Such as "if it costs over $100, he will discuss it with me before making the purchase," or "it is not appropriate to tell casual friends that embarrassing story from my past." Another type of boundary is a tolerance level. In physical measurement, a typical tolerance level could be expressed as "the part is acceptable if its length is

---

65 Accessed on 3/18/21 from: https://www.psychologytoday.com/us/blog/the-hidden-mind/201812/the-automatic-mind (Dec. 19, 2018).

plus or minus .005" of the specified length." Tolerance boundaries are also commonly used in parenting: "If I have to ask you a third time, then…"

Although identifying group membership and establishing boundaries need to be developed, especially if we are to become critical thinkers and good at maintaining relationships, the underlying capability is innate. Remember the newborn who had already defined the "Mom" group membership as the voice with a certain pitch, rhythm, and tenor to her voice and had set the boundary as only that voice.

Many, if not most of our grouping choices are automated; we make them unconsciously. Creating groups, or categories, are essential as we mature and try to manage more and more information. Do you have someone in your life who often begins a new conversation with a pronoun? "She wanted to know if you…." The speaker has in mind who "she" is but the listener often misses the content of the message while trying to figure out the identity of "she."

College students can relate to this when the professor lectures about a topic for which they have no group or category to associate this new information. Until they discover how to place this new information into a context (i.e., a category), they will continue to be unable to process what the teacher is saying. That is why wise teachers begin lectures by announcing the topic (group membership) and how it will relate to information from previous lectures (group boundary).

Creating order through groupings or categories not only makes information meaningful but also provides a type of comfort or security. I am the type of person who likes to have a place for everything and everything in its place. It assures me I'll find that tool in my workshop that I have not used since I can't remember when. Four years after my wife of 44 years passed away, I brought my new wife to my home and gave her the freedom to make it her home. A few weeks later, she had rearranged almost everything in every cabinet, closet, and drawer. We also changed most of the drapes, added shelves to closets, and bought some new furniture. I get it. She was nesting. She was creating new groups and categories to create an order that made sense to her. It made it "her" home. Once I learned her categories, such as "all your off-season clothing goes in this closet," then it became "our" home. Creating her own order to the home's stored items and making some décor choices affirmed her belonging in the home. It made her comfortable and secure.

Some readers may have difficulty relating to this emphasis on keeping an orderly home. They tend to thrive in a chaotic environment. The point is not that order is unimportant to them, but rather they may focus more on the condition of their relationships than the condition of their kitchen counter. They find that building and maintaining relationships is much more important than dirty dishes in the sink or a stack of week's worth of mail on the table. However, when a relationship becomes broken, they find great comfort when the relationship is repaired so that the person belongs again to the previous relationship category and the relationship boundaries are clearly defined and respected.

Other readers may have difficulty relating to either of these types of orders. Both their workspace and relationships may be chaotic, but their focus is progress toward a goal. They are task-oriented people. They find order in effective progress toward some achievement. When the project loses focus or has a setback, they interpret it as a chaos that needs to be re-ordered. The project sequence (i.e., what must be done first, then second, etc., or the tasks that can be done concurrently) is a list of categories. Who is responsible for certain tasks is another list of categories. The boundaries include the due dates, the budget, the quality standards, and the satisfaction of the customer.

Regardless of which type of order is most important to you, separating things, people, or tasks into categories is a part of God-like ruling. It can also be a part of our brokenness. Obsessing over a tidy home or desk while ignoring strained relationships or stalled important tasks is one way of living that does not glorify God. The same is true of living in squalor (think of a teenager's unsupervised room) or not completing homework while spending hours on the phone with friends. The same could be said of working evenings and weekends to get the promotion or win the sale while abusing co-workers and stretching the truth along the way. Paul wrote in 1 Corinthians 14:40, "But everything should be done in a fitting and orderly way." We bring glory to God when we work to bring order to all of our life. That is how God is working even now to restore order to His creation. God-like ruling seeks to bring order by creating and maintaining categories and boundaries. We naturally do it, and yet through the Spirit's transformation, it is one way to become more like the One who designed us.

Diversity in Order

Order is not the same as uniformity. F.F. Bruce commented, "Diversity, not uniformity is the mark of God's handiwork."[66] God ordered His creation but also created immense diversity! God didn't create just ten or twenty kinds of beetles, a few hundred different flowers, or even a thousand kinds of fish. Recent estimates are that there are currently approximately 1,500,000 different species of beetles,[67] 400,000 species

---

66 F.F. Bruce, (1963). The Epistle of Paul to the Romans. In The Tyndale New Testament Commentaries, R.G.V. Tasker, ed. Grand Rapids, MI: Eerdmans. 227.
67 Nigel E. Stork, James McBroom, Claire Gely, and Andrew J. Hamilton (June 1, 2015) New approaches narrow global species estimates for beetles, insects, and terrestrial arthropods. Proceedings of the National Academy of Science of the United States of America. Accessed on 3/20/21 from: https://www.pnas.org/content/112/24/7519

of flowering plants,[68] and 226,000 marine species. These estimates try to include those species as yet undiscovered. Estimates of the number of undiscovered species in the ocean range from a few hundred thousand to more than 10 million.[69] In addition to this immense bio-diversity, individuals within each species are, of course, also a little bit different.

The same is true of our own species. As of March 2021, the world population clock estimates there are 7.9 billion of us now, and each of us is unique.[70] One result of our individual differences is that we each tend to respond to different types of chaos in very different ways. We don't all see the same chaos, and this leads us to seek different types of order, or at least different approaches to creating order out of the chaos. Some of us focus on what is not as it should be and try to fix the brokenness. Others focus on what could be, but is not yet, and try to fulfill the potential.

One of the primary focuses of psychology has been the study of our individual differences. Development, personality, and intelligence have been major topics of research in psychology in an attempt to explain these differences. Theories developed from this research have been widely debated. The point in briefly reviewing some of these

---

68 Lin Edwards (September 23, 2010). Estimate of flowering plant species to be cut by 600,000. Accessed on 3/20/21 from: https://phys.org/news/2010-09-species.html
69 Andy Solow (December, 2012). One Fish, Two Fish: Estimating Undiscovered Species. Accessed 3/20/2021 from: https://ocean.si.edu/ocean-life/one-fish-two-fish-estimating-undiscovered-species
70 www.worldometers.info. (n.d.) Accessed 3/20/21 from: https://www.worldometers.info/world-population/#:~:text=The%20current%20world%20population%20is,Nations%20estimates%20elaborated%20by%20Worldometer

psychological theories is not that this is new information but to show how psychologists have observed individual differences for decades that also help explain different responses to chaos.

Cognitive and Psychosocial Development

Piaget's stage theory of cognitive development proposes that from birth through adolescence, the character of a child's thinking develops from being egocentric (i.e., "It's all about me") to being exocentric (i.e., choices have real consequences from outside forces).[71] Piaget's theory also proposes that as children mature in their thinking, they develop an increased ability to reason with abstract concepts; to consider the possible outcomes of various actions. Both of these transitions will cause differences in how children and adolescents respond to chaos. For instance, a toddler will focus on the chaos that is directly affecting him personally. In contrast, a more cognitively mature person would be more likely to focus on the chaos that is affecting others or society as a whole. Similarly, infants are generally dependent upon others to restore order to their world (i.e., feed them or change their diapers). However, a cognitively mature person would be able to think critically about the consequences of possible solutions and to independently make choices to create order in their world.

Erikson's stage theory of psychosocial development proposed that each stage of life has its own particular chaos to overcome. Remember, chaos can be brokenness, but it can also be a goal yet to be achieved or a solution yet to be discovered. Each of Erikson's eight stages identifies a challenge to our self-image as we relate to or compare ourselves to others. For instance, during elementary school years, Erikson's theory predicts that children who fail to develop competency

---

71 David Myers and Nathan Dewall, Exploring Psychology, 10th edition, (New York: Worth Publishers, 2016), 132.

in some skill compared to their peers will suffer from feelings of inferiority. Later in middle adulthood, Erikson's theory predicts that if, in comparison to others, people judge themselves as not having made life significantly better for the next generation, they will feel their life lacks purpose.[72] Erikson's theory of psychosocial development describes life as a series of challenges to fulfill our potential. In other words, we each start with a realm that is "formless and empty" and are given the opportunity to build a life that is orderly and full. The difference between our ruling strategies will be influenced by our level of cognitive and psychosocial development and also differences in our personality.

Personality

There are several major models of personality, including type theories, trait theories, psychodynamic, behavioral, and humanistic approaches. Of the various trait theories, there are five factors that are common to most of them. These five personality traits seem to provide the most useful information about the difference between personalities.[73] Each of these five traits is a continuum between each personality trait and its opposite. The following chart explains these differences:

---

72 Ibid., 152.
73 P.T. Costa, Jr. and R.R. McCrae. (2011) The five-factor model, five factor theory, and interpersonal psychology. In L.M. Horowitz & S. Strack (Eds.), Handbook of interpersonal psychology: Theory, research, assessment, and therapeutic interventions (pp..91-104). Hoboken, NJ: Wiley.

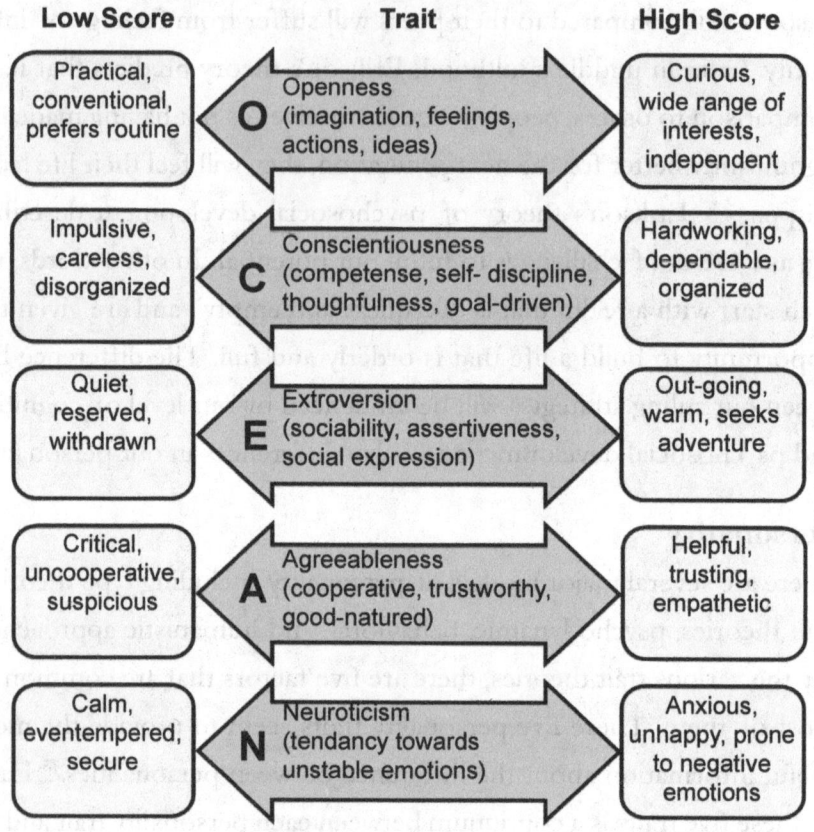

Figure 1. The Five Factor Model[74]

These five factors also influence the type of order a person seeks. For instance, a person who scores high in openness is more likely to seek a new order rather than restoring a previous order. Someone who scores high in agreeableness would prioritize relational order (i.e., a lack of personal conflict) rather than insisting on a better solution. Finally, a person who scores high in conscientiousness would emphasize an external order. They keep their environment organized and their projects on schedule.

---

74 Trait Theorists. (n.d.) Accessed 3/23/2021 from: https://courses.lumenlearning.com/intropsychmaster/chapter/trait-theorists/

Hard-Wired to Separate

Another widely used personality trait model is the DiSC. DiSC is an acronym that stands for the four main personality profiles described in the DiSC model: (D)ominance, (i)nfluence, (S)teadiness and (C)onscientiousness. People with "D" personalities tend to be confident and place an emphasis on accomplishing bottom-line results. People with "i" personalities tend to be more open and place an emphasis on relationships and influencing or persuading others. People with "S" personalities tend to be dependable and place the emphasis on cooperation and sincerity. People with "C" personalities tend to place the emphasis on quality, accuracy, expertise, and competency.[75]

The DiSC personality model illustrates how different personalities define order. Those who score high in influence and steadiness would emphasize harmony in relationships, while those who score high in dominance and conscientiousness would emphasize creating a new order, one that is more effective or efficient. The point is that your unique personality leads you to focus on particular types of chaos and to choose unique strategies to create order.

Other Factors

Several other factors have been used to explain the differences between individuals. These include the warmth of nurturing we received as a child,[76] the culture in which we were raised,[77] our birth order within

---

75 Discprofile.com (n.d.) Accessed on 3/23/21 from: https://www.discprofile.com/what-is-disc/disc-styles
76 R.P. Rohner (1986). The warmth dimension: Foundations of parental acceptance-rejection theory. Newbury Park, CA: Sage.
77 Geert Hofstede (2001). Culture's consequences: Comparing values, behaviors, institutions and organizations across nations. Beverly Hills, CA: Sage.

our nuclear family,[78] the heritability of behaviors,[79] multiple intelligences,[80] and our personal values and beliefs.[81] The list is almost endless. Evangelical Christians would certainly include in this list the status of our relationship to God and our particular spiritual gift(s). Together, all these factors influence the types of order that we seek and the strategies we choose to rule over the chaos in our lives. The resulting diversity among God-like rulers is part of God's design and reflects our likeness to our Creator.

The Greatest Order

Even though we naturally seek to create order in our lives, chaos will continue to rule over us until the greatest source of brokenness is restored. That brokenness is in our relationship with our Creator. Restoration of this relationship begins when we become willing to acknowledge our utter separation from God because of our sin (Romans 3:10-20) and receive God's gracious gift of His righteousness through faith in Jesus Christ (Romans 3:21-26). However, this is just the beginning. Order in our relationship is not restored until our hearts are aligned with God's. In other words, not until what we want is the same as what God wants for us. That requires a significant change in us.

Romans 12:2 says, "Do not conform to the pattern of this world, but be transformed by the renewing of your mind. Then you will be able to test and approve what God's will is—his good, pleasing and perfect will." The first thing to notice in this verse is that there is a

---

78 Kevin Leman (2015). The Birth Order Book: Why You Are The Way You Are. New York: Revell.
79 David Moore (2003). The dependent gene: The fallacy of "nature vs. nurture." New York: Times Books/Henry Holt & Co.
80 Howard Gardner (1999). Multiple views of multiple intelligences. New York: Basic Books.
81 Sagiv L, Roccas S, Cieciuch J, Schwartz SH. Personal values in human life. Nature Human Behaviour. 2017 Sep;1(9):630

"pattern of this world." These are the habits of the mind that are based on the lies of the enemy. Since we hear these lies from many sources, and they are often sweet to our sinful nature, the temptation is to accept them uncritically, to simply conform to them without a struggle.

The second thing to notice in this verse is that the solution is nothing short of transformation. Transformation is not an update of the old self to create "the old self 2.0" but a radical redefinition of who we are. The Greek word translated "transformation" in this passage means "changing inwardly in fundamental character" and is the root of the English term "metamorphosis."[82] The point is that the believer has been given a new "inner reality" that needs to express itself as a new person.

In this verse, the Greek word is a present passive imperative verb. The present tense indicates that it is an on-going process, one that never ends. The passive voice indicates it is something we are to allow to be done to us. Finally, its mood is imperative, which means it is a command. God commands us to open ourselves to the Spirit so that he can re-order our minds. One commentator summed it up this way: Now that we have a new life in the Spirit, we have an obligation to "become what you are."[83]

Third, notice that the transformation occurs through the renewal of our mind. The "mind" Paul is referring to is our God-given capacity to reason, to separate between truth and error. In a sense, our mind has a filter. A mind that conforms to the thinking of this world filters

---

82 Anthony Thiselton. (2017). "The Process of Sanctification" In Devotions on the Greek New Testament, Paul Jackson, ed.) Grand Rapids, MI: Zondervan. 64-64.

83 J. Behm. (1967). "Metamorphoo." in Theological Dictionary of the New Testament. (Botterwick, G.J., Trans.). Grand Rapids, MI: W.B. Eerdmans Publishing Co., IV. 759.

Kings and Queens in the Kingdom of God

out God's truth as foolishness. A renewed mind seeks God's truth and is able to filter out the assumptions of ungodly thinking (1 Corinthians 2:14-16).

The renewed mind is able to "test and approve what God's will is." In other words, to discern God's will and to agree with it. Hodge explained, "The design and result then of that great change of which Paul speaks, is, that Christians should know, delight in, and practice, whatever is good and acceptable to God."[84] The implication is that transformation does not just strengthen our ability to resist temptation; instead, it changes our desires so that what used to tempt us gradually becomes repugnant.

God-like rulers were designed to rule in relationship with God, to be in harmony with His purposes, eager to follow His direction as His beloved and obedient children. This means the things that are most important to God will be a priority for God-like rulers. Instead of focusing on building their own kingdom, God-like rulers will focus on expanding the Kingdom of God. Transformed God-like rulers are able to "participate in the divine nature, having escaped the corruption in the world caused by evil desires" (2 Peter 1:4). How does this participation come about? A God-like ruler who is being transformed becomes a useful tool through which the Spirit can work to affect change in others. We become his agents to spread his light and love to those who need to know them.

In summary, God-like rulers who are being transformed by the Holy Spirit work at subduing chaos in their lives. The renewal of their minds enables them to discern God's will as it relates to the borders of their realm and the ways they are called and gifted to glorify God. Those ways include every aspect of their life, including their relation-

---

84 Charles Hodge. (1886). Commentary on the Epistle to the Romans. Grand Rapids, MI: W.B. Eerdmans Publishing Co., 385.

ships, education, profession, ministry, and hobbies. Every little bit of chaos that is separated into order brings God glory!

God-like rulers whose minds are being renewed recognize that the greatest sources of chaos are the priority. The ongoing process of transformation draws their focus to the chaos in their relationship to God and, out of love for others, the chaos in the brokenness in the world around them. The types of chaos to which they respond and how they choose to address them result from their stage of development, the many personal factors that make each of us unique, and their progress on the journey through the transformation process.

However, identifying the chaos and the order that needs to be established is only the first step of God-like ruling. The emptiness created by the chaos still needs to be filled. The next chapter will discuss how we have been designed to fill the emptiness in our environment, ourselves, and others. We find great joy in filling the emptiness and ultimately this is how we are fulfilled.

Discussion Questions

1. Which is more important to you: The orderliness of your home or office? Or, the peacefulness of your relationships (i.e., lack of "drama')?

2. In what contexts do you have difficulty establishing boundaries to keep others from getting you to do things you'd rather not do? What is it about those contexts, or your relationship with those people that make it difficult for you to establish boundaries?

3. Are you "task-oriented?" What is your typical response when it appears that a due date will be missed or a goal will not be achieved?

4. What area of your life is out of order (i.e., not aligned) with God's will for you? What lie of the enemy is causing you to choose his chaos instead of God's order?

8

Drawn to Fill

There are certain things we all want but are not sure how to get them. Many people search for them their whole life and never succeed. We are attracted to the things that imitate what we want, but we are left empty when the fraud is discovered.

What are these things that everyone wants? First, we want meaning. We want to be meaningful to others, to be loved, needed, and appreciated. Being meaningful to someone could imply that a significant relationship, or at least an emotional bond, has developed. Being meaningful to someone could also mean that we have developed a functional relationship with them. For instance, suppliers, employees, and customers are meaningful to business owners to keep their businesses functioning.

Second, we want purpose. We want our lives to have made a difference, to have changed the world in some lasting way. We hope that something we have accomplished becomes the explanation for why life is better for future generations. Finally, we want our accomplishments to be the result of a well-designed plan and not just a fortuitous accident. That way, our accomplishments give us a sense that we have purpose.

Third, we want value, or more correctly, we want to be valued, to be desired by others. Value can be intrinsic. In other words, something can be valuable for what it is. Often this type of value is based on who created it. An unremarkable pencil sketch might be valuable simply because it was an early work of Leonardo Da Vinci. Or value can be extrinsic. This type of value is based on having what other people want. In a capitalistic economy, value produces power. The greater the desire of others to have what you have or to receive some service you can provide, the greater its value and your power to negotiate.

These three things, meaning, purpose, and value, are what we work for most of our lives, not only because we desire them but also because we often enjoy creating them. Like anything a God-like ruler does, creating meaning and purpose can be done solely for our own glory, for our net worth, or it can be done for the glory of God.

Meaning Makers

We all want our lives to be meaningful. As mentioned in an earlier chapter, there are two kinds of meaning: functional and spatial. Functional meaning enables us to anticipate future events and make decisions accordingly. Spatial meaning defines our personal relationships. We talk of close friends and distant relatives. We place people and things in different relationship categories based on our emotional attachment or level of trust. Examples of relationship categories could be: people I love, people I depend upon, people who depend on me, people I trust enough to do business with, people I disagree with on politics, people I admire but don't know personally, etc. You have probably placed each person you know into multiple categories (e.g., I trust Tom enough to do business with him, I also depend on him, but disagree with him on politics). These categories help us in each situation to act appropriately according to the boundaries we, or our culture, have set.

Most of the meaning we experience is self-generated. We decide for ourselves what people or things mean to us. For the "radah" hypothesis to be correct, there would need to be evidence that God-like rulers ascribe meaning to things and people without being taught to do it. Psychologists have observed that we form perceptions and attachments to order our experiences and make them meaningful. Let's first explore the relationship between perception and meaning.

Rational Meaning: Perception

In the previous chapter, sensation was described as a "bottom-up process" by which we receive information from our environment. Perception, however, is a "top-down process." Our brain tries to order or make sense of the information we are receiving through our senses. John Locke (1632 – 1704) believed that we learn how to perceive through our experiences. Research since Locke indicates that he was partly right. People who were blind at birth, typically with opaque cataracts, after surgery could distinguish light and colors but were unable to tell the difference between a circle and a square. Research on both animals and humans suggests that for normal sensory and perceptual development, there is an optimal period early in our lives when exposure to nurturing experiences is required.[85] Although some nurturing is involved, especially in the first years of life, the ease in which babies learn perceptual skills indicates that we are hard-wired to develop them, just like babies are hard-wired to learn the language they are exposed to.[86]

---

85 David Myers and Nathan Dewall, (2016). Exploring Psychology, 10th edition, (New York: Worth Publishers), 223.
86 Faith Hickman Byrnie, (2009). Brain Sense: The Science of the Senses and How We Process the World Around Us, (New York: AMACOM)

Kings and Queens in the Kingdom of God

Over a century ago, Gestalt psychologists developed the theory that our minds look for associated sensations and then organize them into a "whole" or "gestalt." To do this, Gestalt psychologists discovered a consistent process that we use to bring order to the sensations we are receiving. First, our minds separate between the "figure" and the "ground." The "figure" is whatever we choose to focus our attention on. The "ground" is the background or the sensations we are choosing to ignore. Next, our minds follow certain rules to group the "figure" sensations to perceive a whole that means something to us. Even where those sensations are incomplete, our minds tend to fill in the "gaps" to turn the sensations into meaningful perceptions.[87] For instance, what do you see below?

Do you see three "Pacmen," or do you see a white triangle? That depends on what is the "figure" and what is the "ground." The perception that this is a triangle illustrates the Gestalt law of closure. We fill in the "gaps" to make it mean a triangle even when there is no triangle there.

---

87 David Myers and Nathan Dewall, (2016). Exploring Psychology, 10th edition, (New York: Worth Publishers), 217.

Drawn to Fill

If the universe abhors a vacuum, our mind abhors meaninglessness. One of the repeated experiments I do with my psychology students is to show them the following image and ask them what they see:

I always get several guesses such as a ring, an ear, an eye, and one student who was frustrated that I rejected all their responses, ventured "it must be a black eyed pea." Notice that all the students made it "mean" something. I didn't ask them what it was, or what it was a picture of, I asked them what they saw. Out of hundreds of students, none has ever responded that they see a curved line attached to a big black dot. That is because we naturally ascribe meanings to things, and if we are unsure, we "make" it mean something. Unanswered questions can frustrate us, but solving a mystery or puzzle gives us enjoyment. Finding the meaning or solution gives us the secure feeling that our world is understandable and therefore less scary.

Emotional Meaning: Attachment

The other type of meaning is a type of spatial meaning. In our relationships, spatial meaning is naturally created through attachment, an emotional bonding to someone or something. In essence, an attachment is naturally created when a person or thing makes us feel secure. Children become attached to familiar people and things. Just being repeatedly exposed to people or things develops a fondness because familiarity provides a sense of security. That is why small children become attached to blankets and stuffed toys and why they like you to read to them the same books over and over.[88]

Adults may also be attached to people or things because they remind them of safe times in their past, because they hold the potential to protect them in the future, or perhaps because of the level of personal investment they have in the person or thing. If they have invested a lot of money, time, or their reputation on something, it is too threatening to their self-esteem to admit that they might have been unwise. They will remain emotionally attached to their belief despite evidence to the contrary.

Levels of attachment to people or things create general relationship categories with boundaries. We don't assign a specific attachment value but place people into general categories such as your lover, best friends, family, casual friends, acquaintances, etc. Our relationship to things or people is defined by the category into which we have placed them. Separating our relationships into categories is one way we bring order to our life.

There are several ways we create emotional bonds with people: eye contact, touch, feeding, and sharing intimacy, for instance. By "intimacy," I don't necessarily mean sex. Something is "intimate" when it makes us vulnerable. Emotional intimacy is when we share our feelings with others who we trust will not judge us or take advantage of our vulnerability. Experiencing intimacy with others fills a significant need in our life. It means that we are not alone in our feelings and experiences, that we have a "safe place" to talk about our questions, and that we are valued by someone for who we are.[89]

---

88 Ibid, 139.
89 Laurenceau, J.-P., & Kleinman, B. M. (2006). Intimacy in Personal Relationships. In A. L. Vangelisti & D. Perlman (Eds.), The Cambridge handbook of personal relationships (p. 637–653). Cambridge University Press. https://doi.org/10.1017/CBO9780511606632.035

God-like rulers are designed to be meaning makers. We naturally organize our perceptions onto meaningful wholes. We also innately develop emotional attachments to people and things who make us feel safe. We do this because we need our life to make sense, to have meaning to us. Attachment is what other people and things mean to us. However, there is another type of meaning that we seek. That is the meaning we have to others.

By becoming meaningful to someone who is significant to us or by being a significant part of something bigger than us, we feel our life has meaning. Of course, this assumes that this "something bigger than us" will last. However, when that person or thing we've tied our life's meaning to is gone, so is the meaning of our life. That is why Christians ultimately find meaning by being part of the never-ending Kingdom of God.

The Power and Problem of Purpose

We are, and always have been, goal setters, from the infant who is determined to crawl to the toy she wants to the middle-aged couple who are setting goals for their retirement, deciding what we want, and going after it is a natural part of life. However, goal setting is a skill that also needs to be developed.

Many people are poor goal setters. Early in the elementary school years, some children take a defensive role in setting goals. After challenges come their way (think of school work, homework, and chores), they procrastinate for as long as they can. For them, a successful day is when they can avoid responsibilities or give minimal effort until the bell rings and they are out of school for the day. Later in life, the goal is to make it through the workweek till Friday, doing enough to avoid getting fired. Poor goal-setters have never grown out of this defensive posture.

More mature goal-setters move into an offensive role towards goal-setting. They not only anticipate challenges and pro-actively work to solve or even prevent them, but they also create new challenges by visioning a better world for themselves and others. Every new vision creates the challenges of design (purpose, features, and benefits), resources (expertise, time, and money), measurement (defining how to measure success), and leadership (finding a way to get it done). These challenges energize mature goal-setters. They simply break down each of these challenges into specific tasks, delegate the tasks to either themselves or someone else, and set a reasonable due date for their completion.

Richard Leider, in his popular book, "The Power of Purpose," explains there is a difference between setting goals and finding your purpose in life, "I needed to embrace the "why?" of purpose before I selected the "what?" of my goals."[90] He notes that focusing on goals without considering the overall purpose of your life ultimately results in a life of meaningless busyness. His thesis is that clarifying your life's purpose is a powerful motivator, the reason to get up in the morning and to persevere when the going gets tough.

Leider's strategy for finding your life's purpose includes three steps: unlocking your story, your gifts, and your curiosity. Unlocking your story means identifying a need you can fill, especially if your experiences have prepared you to meet that need. Unlocking your gifts means identifying your talents that would be helpful to meet that need. Leider views our talents as gifts to be given to the world. Unlocking your curiosity means identifying the passion that causes you to desire to learn more about it.

---

90 Richard Leider. (2015). The Power of Purpose, Find meaning, live longer, better. (Oakland, CA: Berrett-Koehler Publishers), 22.

Drawn to Fill

Trying to choose your own purpose has a way of ending badly, especially when it follows this cycle:
1. You discover what you are good at in comparison to others
2. Doing what you are good at brings accolades from others
3. Being recognized for what you do feeds your passion for doing it more
4. Being talented and passionate about something leads you to believe it is your life's purpose
5. One day, you are no longer receiving accolades from others
6. Without the recognition, your passion fades
7. You lose a sense of purpose for your life

This cycle is especially familiar to professional athletes, Hollywood starlets, and retirees who have passed their prime. Drug addiction, depression, and many failed relationships are all too common for those who choose a life's purpose based on how well they compare to others. However, not everyone who chooses their purpose based on their talents and passion has this experience, especially those who see their talents as gifts to be given to others who need what their talents can provide.

Lastly, Leider explains that your life purpose changes as you mature. He used the metaphor of a spiral staircase. Our life's purpose constantly advances, changing as we mature through the stages of life while winding around a core value. He recommends a core value of compassion for others.

This all sounds good except for one thing. It's godless. Of course, he appeals to the scriptures of various religions and their common command to love your neighbor, but in the end, each person is the captain of their ship who alone defines his own purpose. In Leider's view, living out your purpose tells the story of you rather than the story of God's glory. As you recall from Psalm 19, all creation is telling the story of God's glory. That includes us. So just like the rest of creation, the ultimate purpose of the human race is to bring glory to God. The purpose of your individual life is to tell your unique part of the grand story, a part that was designed for you, and no one else can tell it.

In Handel's oratorio, Messiah, Jesus is proclaimed to be "King of Kings, and Lord of Lords." Handel may have gotten this from Revelation 1:5, which says that Jesus is "the ruler of the kings of the earth." Since God designed you to be a ruler, you are a king, and God has prepared a realm for you to rule. Ephesians 2:10 says, "For we are God's handiwork, created in Christ Jesus to do good works, which God prepared in advance for us to do." So, if we follow Christ and make Him the Lord of our life, our purpose is not ours to choose but ours to receive. Your purpose is to rule in a God-like way over the realm God has given you so as to tell your story about the glory of God.

Of course, your gifts, including both natural talents, spiritual gifts, and your passion, are clues to the realm God has prepared for you to rule. However, the specific realm God has for you at every stage of life is clarified in your relationship with Him. He is our Shepherd. We, His sheep, hear His voice and follow Him (John 10:27). Being confident of God's call on your life, each day asking for and listening in prayer for direction, gives us great confidence that we are using our time and resources for God's glory. Leider is correct; knowing your purpose is a powerful motivator!

So, if knowing our purpose is a powerful source of motivation, what is the problem? Quite simply, it is also a major source of temptation. Our sinful nature wants to expand our realm beyond the limits given to us in scripture (e.g., ruling over people rather than ruling over our environment). Our corrupted nature wants to build OUR kingdom for OUR glory rather than build the kingdom of God within the realm given us for God's glory.

Beyond just setting goals for ourselves and achieving them, we want our life to have a purpose. You could decide your purpose is to build your kingdom for your glory. Such kingdoms will last only a moment in light of eternity. Or, you could invest in building the eternal Kingdom of God. 1 Corinthians 3:11-15 warns us,

> For no one can lay any foundation other than the one already laid, which is Jesus Christ. If anyone builds on this foundation using gold, silver, costly stones, wood, hay or straw, their work will be shown for what it is, because the Day will bring it to light. It will be revealed with fire, and the fire will test the quality of each person's work. If what has been built survives, the builder will receive a reward. If it is burned up, the builder will suffer loss but yet will be saved—even though only as one escaping through the flames.

The Creation of Value

When I asked a realtor what the value of my home was, he said, "It is worth whatever someone is willing to pay for it." In other words, the value is determined by the buyer, not by the seller. Of course, the seller can price the home as high as they want, but it is only worth what buyers are willing to pay. Putting a value on something is a personal decision that is based on the thing's meaning and purpose for you.

When people or things are meaningful to us, or if we believe they will help us achieve our purposes, we assign value to them. A new home purchase is often based on what the new home means to the buyers. It may affirm to them that they have reached a new social economic level. It could also mean that they will now have room to expand their family or that they have made a commitment to stay in the area for an extended time.

Kings and Queens in the Kingdom of God

Assigning value to things comes naturally to us, just as ascribing meaning and establishing purposes, stem from how God designed us. We can value things on an emotional level, an instrumental level, or, more likely, a combination of both. Realtors and home sellers love it when a buyer becomes emotionally attached to the house for sale. It increases the value to the buyers and thus the price they are willing to pay.

We also value things based on their importance to help us achieve one or more of our goals. Sometimes there may be something that is both necessary and sufficient for us to succeed. If success in that goal is important to us, we will assign a high value to it. For other goals, the same thing might be merely helpful but not necessary. Then, its value to us is less. When our goal is not clearly defined, we are not sure what we want to accomplish, the importance of something for our success is also unclear, making a value judgment more difficult.

How is value created? Essentially, whenever you turn chaos into order or make someone or something meaningful to you or others, or helpful in achieving a purpose, you have created value. The factors of order, meaning, and purpose are the basis of value in our economy. Forests, iron ore, and crude oil are examples of raw materials that need to be separated into a more orderly state, such as lumber, steel, and gasoline. Marketers work to increase the meaning of the product or service. A deodorant is not just a way to smell good; it is a powerful strategy to attract the opposite sex. A bowl of cereal is not just breakfast; it means you are a good parent if you feed it to your children. Designers of products work to increase the product's functionality to fulfill more of the consumer's goals. That is why cup holders in cars have suddenly multiplied. The auto industry discovered that some people value a vehicle in part by how many cup holders it has. Soccer moms, for instance, tend to want to keep their cars clean and need a cup holder for every passenger for that purpose.

Take a moment to analyze what you do as an employee to create value for your company. You will find that every task you do to facilitate the sale of your company's product or service can be broken down into either creating order, meaning, or purpose for the customer. Of course, in companies with multiple departments, your customer may be the internal department that receives from you the products or information that you produce. If a task produces something that isn't meaningful or useful for your customer, then that task is probably unnecessary. Worse than that, it robs your company of resources that could have been used to make your product, or service more valuable to your customer and your company more profitable. Identifying and eliminating processes that create little to no value for the customer is easier said than done.

Our modern economy is very complex and highly specialized. Most of us contribute only a small part of the whole process required to bring value to the customer. Think of the difference between modern family life and a family living in the wilderness. Imagine having to provide everything you need to survive without the outside world's help. They would have to grow their food, make their tools and clothing, build their shelter, and create their community. They would have to start with raw materials and separate them to create order (e.g., separate the grain from the wheat, separate the meat from the carcass, separate the board from the tree). Then they would have to process the usable material to create meaning or purpose with it (e.g., wheat berries become bread, the meat becomes a steak dinner, a board becomes a tabletop). But in the modern world, almost everything comes to us ordered (designed, manufactured, packaged, and transported) for our meaning and purposes. Your job and mine is just one cog in the massive process of creating the order, meaning, and purpose that customers will value. Your value to the company is determined by the company's judgment of the amount of order, meaning, and purpose you contribute to the product or service they sell.

For homemakers, the frequent tasks you do create order (e.g., shopping, organizing, and cleaning), meaning (e.g., training your children, comforting them, and making memories), and purpose (meeting the needs of your family members). When I teach, I am trying to create order in my student's minds by creating categories of the information so it will be understandable. I could just spout off a list of facts, but by separating them into topics, I pre-order the information so that they can capture the meaning and purpose of the information. Then I try to provide an illustration to make the information meaningful to the student and explain how it will help them achieve future goals.

There is yet another external valuation and one that is most important. I mentioned above that how much others value us is still a personal judgment. It is our estimation of how we are valued by others rather than how they actually value us. Like any judgment, we can be wrong. The valuation I'm referring to is God's valuation of you. Does he love you? Do you mean anything to him? Does he have a purpose for your life? Perhaps the best answer to these questions can be found in Philippians 2:6-8, where Paul explains how much Jesus was willing to pay to re-establish a relationship with you:

> [6] Who, being in very nature God,
>
> did not consider equality with God something to be used to his own advantage;
>
> [7] rather, he made himself nothing
>
> by taking the very nature of a servant,
>
> being made in human likeness.
>
> [8] And being found in appearance as a man,

Drawn to Fill

> he humbled himself
> by becoming obedient to death—
> even death on a cross!

We receive many clues from many different voices on how much they value us. The question is, whose valuation do we value the most. Do we trust our feelings of how valuable we are? Do we trust the feedback we receive from other people about our value? Or, do we trust God's declaration of our value to Him? Whose value judgment we value the most is our Lord, the one we serve. It also determines whether, after sinning, we run from Him or run to Him.

In summary, we are designed to fill our environment with meaning, purpose, and value. God-like rulers who are being transformed by the Holy Spirit assign meaning through our renewed mind's perceptions and the level of attachment we assign to people and things based on the value God places on them. We set goals to accomplish the unique purpose we have received through the will of God. Finally, we create value when we make people or things more meaningful or purposeful for others. God created God-like rulers to tell part of the story of His glory. Filling our environment with meaning, purpose, and value is how we tell this story.

Kings and Queens in the Kingdom of God

Discussion Questions

1. What relationships bring spatial or emotional meaning to you (i.e., makes you feel loved, needed, and appreciated)?

2. Name some people with whom you have a functionally meaningful relationship (i.e., They are dependent upon you, or you are dependent upon them)? Which of those you named also bring you spatial or emotional meaning?

3. How might you discover that you were trying to rule over something that was not in the realm God had given you?

4. What are some of the "voices" in your life that tell you that you are valued? What "voices" tell you the opposite?

9

Take Your Rightful Throne

You and I were created to rule, but we have been deceived into ascending to the wrong throne. As soon as we were old enough to begin asserting our will, we took over the throne of our heart, insisting on or scheming to get what we wanted. But, that throne is God's alone. He insists, and rightly so, to be the King of kings and the Good Shephard of our souls. To begin a relationship with God, we must first relinquish the throne of our heart and acknowledge Him as our Lord.

Even worse than trying to rule ourselves, however, we sometimes try to rule other people. Attempting to rule others comes in many forms. The legalist attempts to control you by telling you, for example, what types of clothing or media are not acceptable to God. The emotionally manipulative person tries to control you by making you feel the way He wants you to feel. The violent person intends to control you through intimidation, and if that doesn't work, through physical force. The liar seeks to control your perception of the truth. The thief chooses to overrule your property rights. The gossip presumes control over your privacy. There are many thrones that are not ours to ascend.

Kings and Queens in the Kingdom of God

Trying to rule outside the boundaries of the realm He has given us weighs us down with worries we were not created to bear. After relinquishing the control of my life to God, I became free to begin focusing on the throne from which God intended me to rule. However, this leads to new decisions that must be made, for instance, accepting my responsibility to rule rather than flaking out and trying to push my responsibilities onto others. For example, a college student wore a tee-shirt on campus the other day that said, "I can't "adult" today." I guess he was hoping someone would follow him around, repeatedly reminding him of what he needs to do.

Taking the responsibility to rule also means identifying the borders of my realm. This means focusing on what I am responsible for instead of pointing fingers at what others are not doing that I think they should do. It means recognizing what God has called me to do and not trying to do what God has called others to do. As Steven Covey put it, "Focus on your circle of influence rather than your circle of concern."[91] There are a lot of things I am concerned about but have no influence over. Focusing on those things within the boundaries of my realm keeps me from wasting time and energy and creating personal conflicts in the process.

We can choose to rule over our realm by ourselves in isolation from God. Or, we can choose to rule over our realm by participating with God (2 Peter 1:4), asking for His leading and wisdom (Proverbs 3:6; 4:11, James 1:5), and depending on His strength and provision to create value in and for others (Philippians 4:13; 4:19). In our individualistic culture, we also tend to choose to rule in isolation from others. In reality, most of our realms are responsibilities we share with others.

---

91 Steven Covey, (1980). The Seven Habits of Highly Effective People. New York: Simon and Schuster.

Therefore, the boundaries of our realms blend with and overlap the realms of those who are working with us toward the same goal.

But submitting to His rule over us does not mean there is nothing left for us to rule. He has given you and me a realm, a context, in which we have free will to rule. That realm includes all our relationships and responsibilities. In our relationships, rather than rule over the will of other people, we can create order in our relationships by establishing priorities and boundaries. Then we can choose to fill others with meaning, purpose, and value. Dave Ferguson recommends to disciple-makers a short phrase, "I see in you…" as a means of encouraging those who are growing in the Lord and helping them discover their spiritual gift or calling.[92] That is just one example of filling someone with meaning, purpose, and value.

Another example, is how I rule over my marriage. That does not mean that I insist my wife submit to me. Instead, it means that I make her my highest priority, that I keep myself only for her. Ruling over my marriage involves blessing her by repeatedly telling her what she means to me and how much I value her. It also requires my understanding of her goals and priorities to support her and help her accomplish them. Ruling over my marriage is not about ruling over my wife. It's how I rule over the way I relate to her and how I continue to "marry" her (i.e., become one with her).

In our responsibilities, to rule over my environment means physically separating things to create the type of order that fills those things with meaning, purpose, and value. This happens in as many different ways as there are professions. For example, a lumberjack separates a tree from its limbs and roots so that it can be hauled to the sawmill. The truck driver hauls logs to the mill (i.e., separates it from the for-

---

92 Dave Ferguson (2018). Hero Maker, Five essential practices for leaders to multiply leaders. Grand Rapids, MI: Zondervan. pp. 141-142.

est) so that the tree can be separated into lumber. Now the wood of the tree is meaningful for the purpose of building a house. The tree's wood now has value to the home builder and ultimately to the family who will buy the home.

Similar scenarios could be outlined in various other professions. Physicians work to separate all possible causes of my symptoms and then to separate the most effective treatment from other possible treatments to separate us from disease. Teachers help students separate right from wrong (e.g., two plus two does not equal five) and fill learning opportunities with meaningful experiences to learn the skills that will increase their value to society. Accountants separate raw data into categories to make meaning of the numbers and provide valuable information to the management. Production managers schedule production processes in an orderly sequence to make a product that will be meaningful to the customer because it will help them accomplish their purpose. Creating something which others value and therefore are willing to pay for is capitalism. When all of this is done with integrity, respect for one another, and careful stewardship of our resources, it glorifies the God who designed us to rule over our environment.

Accept Your Responsibility to Rule

Because of technology and globalization, we live in a very complex world. Simple solutions touted by politicians and pundits are enticing but are almost always wrong or incomplete. Our 24-hour global news media also confront us with wars, corruption, poverty, slavery, riots, and natural disasters from every corner of the globe. Like the average citizen, I am tempted to withdraw from all the noise and let the "experts" solve the problems. It is wise to avoid speaking into issues you do not understand, but on the other hand, if good people do nothing, then evil will prevail. At least I need to be an informed voter and communicate my concerns to my representatives in the government.

Trying to be informed on the issues can be exhausting, especially when the biases of our sources cause conflicting narratives. How do you decide who to believe? Frustrated and uncertain, many choose to withdraw from the conversation. They retreat to what I call the "castle mentality." They build walls around their "world" and take a defensive posture to the problems that are "out there." Those walls could be literal, as in gated communities, or they may be metaphorical, such as choosing to ignore the news, staying away from social media, and choosing not to let scripture challenge them. Inside their "castle walls," they typically shrink their world to only those things that most people desire, namely personal peace and prosperity.

However, as a believer, I know I have been called to rule for the glory of God. Every ruler is responsible for a realm made up of many small realms or responsibilities. But, what is my realm? What am I supposed to rule? Your realm is the extent of your influence and responsibility. Is it up to God or me to identify my realm? Paul told the Athenians, "From one man he made all the nations, that they should inhabit the whole earth; and he marked out their appointed times in history and the boundaries of their lands" (Acts 17:26). This verse indicates that you and I aren't living when and where we are by chance. We also know that within the context God has placed us, He has prepared good works for us to do (Ephesians 2:10). So God has designed a time, place, and purpose for your ruling. He has also given you spiritual gifts, natural talents, and unique experiences to equip you to do those good works. Finally, He has given you positions of authority. Examples include your title and job description at work, your parenting role, your finances, and the stewardship of everything you own. Together, they define the boundaries of your realm. The question is whether or not you will accept the responsibility to rule over the realm that God has given you. Are you willing to focus on what God has called you to do (i.e., your realm) and trust Him to take care of everything else?

Discover your realm

So, what is your realm? Whatever it is, it will include chaos that needs to be ordered. People and things within your realm will need to be given new meaning and purpose. Your realm will hold potential for value but will need to be filled. Frankly, it will be a mess. That is because it needs the gifts and talents God has given you to rule. But how do I identify my realm? One strategy is to follow the maxim, "form follows function." In other words, the function or purpose of a thing can be discovered by observing the features of its design. The purpose of a fork can be distinguished from the purpose of a spoon by noting the differences in its shape. If something is designed for a purpose, then the final shape is chosen for effectiveness in accomplishing that purpose.

Earlier, I introduced Richard Leider's strategy for finding your life's purpose.[93] It included three steps: identifying a need you can fill, identifying your talents that would be helpful to meet that need, and identifying the passion that causes you to desire to learn more about it. This strategy essentially follows the "form follows function" maxim. There are a few reasons why this strategy is not sufficient for identifying your realm. First, your purpose and your realm are not the same things. Our purpose is to glorify God by being God-like rulers. This is universally true of all humans and for all time. But your realm is where you, and you alone, have been called to display your God-like ruling at the present time. So, our purpose is the same for all of us, but

---

93 Richard Leider. (2015). The Power of Purpose, Find meaning, live longer, better. (Oakland, CA: Berrett-Koehler Publishers).

your realm is unique to you and to the current situation in which God has placed you.

The second reason why Leider's strategy is insufficient is that it is godless. In other words, it does not acknowledge God's lordship over our discovery process. He appeals to religion for his core moral value (loving your neighbor) but does not conceive of seeking God's direction when identifying our purpose. Jesus is our Shepherd, and we are to listen for his voice and follow him (John 10:27). Listening and following is how we live in fellowship with Jesus. The Apostle John explained this in terms of walking in God's light,

> This is the message we have heard from him and declare to you: God is light; in him there is no darkness at all. If we claim to have fellowship with him and yet walk in the darkness, we lie and do not live out the truth. But if we walk in the light, as he is in the light, we have fellowship with one another, and the blood of Jesus, his Son, purifies us from all sin. (1 John 1:5-7)

If you want to discover the realm God has given you, then you need to ask Him to lead you to it and reveal every part of it to you. He wants you to find your unique part in the story of God's glory. He also wants you to be transformed from a corrupt ruler who seeks his own glory to a God-like ruler who seeks to rule for the glory of God. Your God-like ruling over your specific realm is just one small part of the grand epic referred to in Psalm 19.

How do you discover the borders of your realm? First, you must learn to separate between the voice of God and all the other "voices" from your culture, your friends and teachers, and even your assumptions that are trying to influence you. On the Mount of Transfiguration (see Matthew 17:1-13), Peter was so full of himself and his assumptions of how he could help that he was missing the entire meaning of the experience. God interrupted Peter and said, "This is my Son, whom I love; with him I am well pleased. Listen to him!" If we want to avoid Peter's folly, then we must learn how to listen. For me, that begins with listening to what he has already said in the Bible—not only about what attitudes and behaviors are right or wrong—but also about the character of God's will and how we can discern it.

The distinction between God's purpose for everyone and His will for individuals at a particular time is made clear by three Greek words in the New Testament. The first, "boulae" refers to the decrees of God before the creation of the world (Ephesians 1:3-12). These decrees were God's decisions on what to create and how He would relate to His creation before He said, "Let there be light."[94] God's "boulae" was not only decided in eternity past but also will never change in the future (Hebrews 6:17).[95]

The second word, "prothesin" is a synonym of "boulae." Paul consistently uses "prothesin" to refer to the "primal decision of God whereby the saving event in Christ and the resultant community… are established and set into motion."[96] 2 Timothy 1:9-10 provides an example of how this word is used,

> He has saved us and called us to a holy life—not because of anything we have done but because of his own purpose ("prothesin") and grace. This grace was given us in Christ Jesus before the beginning of time, but it has now been revealed through the appearing of our Savior, Christ Jesus, who has

---

[94] Henry Thiessen (1979), Lectures in Systematic Theology Revised by Vernon Doerksen. (Grand Rapids, MI: W.B. Eerdmans), 104-110.

[95] Gottlob Schrenk. Theological Dictionary of the New Testament., Eds. G. Kittle and G. Fredrich. 1972. (Grand Rapids, MI: W.B. Eerdmans) Vol I, 636.

[96] Christian Maurer. Theological Dictionary of the New Testament., Eds. G. Kittle and G. Fredrich. 1972. (Grand Rapids, MI: W.B. Eerdmans) Vol VII, 166.

destroyed death and has brought life and immortality to light through the gospel.

The third word "thelaema" stands in contrast to both "boulae" and "prothesin." God's will (thelaema), is not the same for everyone. Paul notes that he was called to be an apostle by God's will (thelaema); however, his helpers were not. He also prays for the Colossians that God would fill them with "the knowledge of his will (thelaema) through all the wisdom and understanding that the Spirit gives," (Colossians 1:9). This indicates that God's "thelaema" is communicated to individuals and congregations through their personal relationship with God and the leading of the Spirit.

That God's "boulae," "prothesin," and "thelaema" work in harmony is confirmed by Ephesians 1:11-12,

> In him we were also chosen, having been predestined according to the plan (prothesin) of him who works out everything in conformity with the purpose (boulae) of his will (thelaema), in order that we, who were the first to put our hope in Christ, might be for the praise of his glory."

So God's eternal and unchanging purpose for creating and then redeeming His fallen creation was established before the creation of the world and this universal purpose for all of creation is "once for all" (Jude 3) revealed in His Word.

God further specified His purpose (boulae) for the human race, the "God-like rulers" in Genesis 1:26-28. However, His will (thelaema) for each one of us, which changes as we go through life's stages, is only known through communion with God through the Holy Spirit. Therefore, our purpose is to glorify God by ruling over our realm as God would. However, God's will (thelaema) for you in particular and for this season of your life (i.e., your realm) is something only you can discover through your knowledge of yourself and with the wisdom that God generously gives (James 1:5). Pray for that wisdom and then patiently listen! The enemy often says to us "hurry up" but more often God says "wait".

There is no formula or methodology for discovering what your realm includes; however, there are some biblical principles that should set boundaries for your discovery process. The first principle is that God's thelaema never conflicts with God's word. God will never tell you to do something that the Bible teaches not to do. Therefore, if you want to be skillful in knowing what is or is not in your realm, you need to become familiar with what the Bible reveals to us. A second principle is that God is present with us. He is not far off and unavailable (Acts 17:27-28). He has not left us to figure it out on our own (Matthew 28:20). Proverbs 3:5-6 warns us against depending solely upon our own reasoning,

> Trust in the Lord with all your heart
> and lean not on your own understanding;
> in all your ways submit to him,
> and he will make your paths straight.

This passage does not say that there is no reasonableness to God's leading, but rather we must not put the full weight of our decision or "lean upon" our own understanding. Of course, your spiritual gifts, talents, personality, education, experience, and passion are factors to consider. However, in my life, God has led me in directions that at the time did not make sense to me in light of these factors. Only years later did I realize that God was preparing me for a ministry that I could never have anticipated.

A third biblical principle is that God is never late, nor ever in a hurry. Ecclesiastes 3:11 reminds us, "He has made everything beautiful in its time." There are two kinds of time mentioned in the Bible. "Chronos" time is time measure by the movement of the sun, moon, and stars. This is the time measured by my watch and calendar. The other type of time written about in the Bible is "kairos" time. This time, often translated as the "fullness of time" or "the proper season," is measured by the fulfillment or completion of a process such as grain or fruit ripening (Matthew 13:30; 16:3; 21:34). Any farmer will tell you that they cannot schedule in advance when he will harvest his grain. The farmer watches his fields, not his calendar. The point is that God will reveal changes to His will (thelaema) at the proper (kairos) time as he leads you. That is why we are repeatedly encouraged in scripture to "wait upon the Lord" (Psalm 37:9; 123:2, Isaiah 30:18; 40:31, Jeremiah 14:22, Lamentations 3:25-26, Zephaniah 3:8). As long as you are actively listening to what God is telling you, focus on the current realm of responsibilities He has given you.

These three biblical principles will guide you when you sense God is leading you to rule over a new realm, but there are relationships and responsibilities that are in all of our realms throughout our lives. The Bible has much to say about these. The following is a shortlist of areas the Bible speaks to in all of our realms. I also provide a limited list of some scripture passages relating to each topic to encourage you to explore them further.

1. My Heart (Proverbs 4:23, Matthew 15:1-20, Matthew 22:37, 2 Corinthians 4:16, Ephesians 1:18, Philippians 4:6-7, Colossians 3:1-17, 2 Timothy 2:22, Hebrews 3:7-19, James 4:8, I John 3:19-22)
2. My Relationships (Romans 12:9-21, 1 Corinthians 13, Ephesians 5:21-6:9, Philippians 2:1-11.
3. My Commitments (Proverbs 16:1-3, Matthew 5:31-37, Colossians 3:22-24, James 4:13-17)
4. My Health (1 Corinthians 6:19, Ephesians 5:29, 1 Timothy 4:8, 3 John 1:2)

5. My Learning (Proverbs 1:1-7, 1 Timothy 4:13-16, 2 Timothy 2:15)
6. My Career and Finances (Matthew 6:19-34, Mark 12:13-17; 12:41-44; Luke 10:25-37, Romans 13:7-8)
7. My Witness (1 Peter 3:15, 1 Corinthians 6:1-6, 1 Thessalonians 4:9-12, 1 Timothy 3:7, 2 Timothy 1:8)

Remember that God-like ruling in each of these areas means to make them the right priority for you at this time (i.e., to order them) and then fill them with meaning and purpose in order to create value. There is no need to get anxious about discovering your realm (Philippians 4:6). If we are seeking His direction, He will make it clear to us at the proper time in what circumstances He wants us to use our influence to create order, meaning, purpose, and value.

Rule Your Realm to Glorify God

So, here you are. You are living, and working, going to school, or retired, in a particular community and culture. You have had unique experiences and opportunities that have shaped you. You also have natural talents that have enabled you to take advantage of those experiences and opportunities to prepare you for doing all that you do now. If you have invited Jesus to be your Lord and Savior, then you were also marked with a seal, the promised Holy Spirit (Ephesians 1:13-14). When the Holy Spirit came to reside in your heart, you received a spiritual gift that enables you to meet the spiritual needs of others (Romans 12:3-6, I Peter 4:10-11, I Corinthians 4:4-11).

Now you have a bundle of capabilities that have equipped you to rule over the realm God has given you. That realm includes all of your relationships and responsibilities. The question is, "How do I use my capabilities for the Glory of God?" Jesus answered this question in Matthew 6:33, "But seek first his kingdom and his righteousness, and all these things will be given to you as well." In other words, focus first on being who God wants you to be rather than doing stuff for God.

Seeking to align your life with Jesus' teachings on the Kingdom of God is the first place to begin ruling your realm. Now might be a good time to assess your realm to evaluate what parts might need to be reprioritized and given to the Lord to rule. Appendix B contains a list of coaching questions to help you identify all that God has given you to rule. Appendix C is a guide for God-like ruling in a particular situation. Addressing these issues will make you more useful to God and to others.

Remember, whenever you change a chaotic or empty situation so that it is orderly and full of meaning and purpose, you glorify God. If you find ways to make your job more effective or efficient or your products or services more valuable, you glorify God. If your family moves into a different house and you fill it with love and memories, you glorify God. If you mentor a child who is struggling in school, you glorify God. If you wash the dishes and put them away, you glorify God. If you repair a broken vehicle back to safety and reliability, you glorify God. If you help two friends who are at odds restore their relationship, you glorify God.

These actions can all glorify God, especially if they become a testimony to others of a life that can have meaning and purpose. The greatest order and filling is when we help others find their way back to God. This type of ordering and filling will last for eternity. But note that all of these situations described above had at some point become chaotic and empty of meaning and purpose. If we are to be God-like rulers, we will need to venture out of our neatly ordered castle and enter into the chaos. That's what Jesus did for us when He left heaven and found Himself in the broken world of the Jews and the Romans (Philippians 2:6-11).

On the other hand, you could also do all these things just to build your own wealth and influence in your community. If this is your motive, then you get the glory, not God. The difference is whether you are doing these things to affirm yourself or you do them strategically to let your faith shine through these deeds to give God the glory. Jesus taught in Matthew 5:16: "In the same way, let your light shine before others, that they may see your good deeds and glorify your Father in heaven."

Filling and being filled is one of the major themes in the book of Ephesians. Apostle Paul explained, "And God placed all things under his feet and appointed him to be head over everything for the church, which is his body, the fullness of him who fills everything in every way" (Ephesians 1:22-23). This is interesting. The church is the fullness of Jesus, and He, by the end of this redemption story, will have filled "everything in every way" (including us) with meaning, purpose, and value. Once more, He will be able to say of all creation, "It is very good." In Ephesians 3:19, Paul prays, "that you may be filled to the measure of all the fullness of God." The goal of the believer's ministry is that they might fill each other until they attain "to the whole measure of the fullness of Christ." Just like Christ, we are fulfilled when we fill others.

Call to Action

The "radah" hypothesis states that we were created in the image and likeness of God. Part of that likeness is ruling as God rules. God-like ruling is the human part of the story of God's glory. God-like ruling was corrupted through Adam's sin, and "ruling" came to mean to force one's will upon other people. Through Christ's redemption, our ruling can be restored to what God intended.

Take Your Rightful Throne

God-like rulers are what we are being redeemed to be. We are fallen God-like rulers who repeatedly turn away from God's will by seeking to build our realm for our own glory. While we work to subdue the chaos around us by creating order in our realms and filling them with meaning, purpose, and value, we are also being transformed by God. He is subduing the chaos in us by the renewing of our minds (Romans 12:2) so that by God's grace, we will let God fill our emptiness with the fullness of Christ (Ephesians 4:13, Colossians 2:9-10).

God-like ruling separates or distinguishes to create order where there was chaos and fills the new order with meaning and purpose where there was emptiness. This process adds value to people and things. However, we are to rule only in the realm in which God has given us the freedom to rule. As we submit our realm to God's lordship and take full advantage of His leading and provision, our God-like ruling fills God (We are "the fullness of him who fills everything in every way" Ephesians 1:23). When we tell our part of the story of His glory, it also fulfills us by fulfilling the purpose for which we were created. It is God's will that you be fulfilled by doing what He designed you to do. Seeking true fulfillment is not a selfish act. It is the result of bringing glory to God by being God-like rulers as God designed us to be.

Kings and Queens in the Kingdom of God

Discussion Questions

1. When physically ruling over our environment is done with integrity, respect for one another, and careful stewardship of our resources, I claimed it glorifies God. Are there other criteria for physically ruling that should also be considered?

2. What were some legalistic rules (requirements or restrictions not specified in the Bible) you were raised to follow?

3. What does a "castle mentality" look like in your faith community?

4. Reflect on your heritage and major life experiences. What do they tell you about the possible realm God might have given you at this point in your life?

Kings and Queens in the Kingdom of God

5. What are some chaotic situations that God might be calling you to bring His order?

10

Rule in Harmony With Others

When I was around six years old, my parents drove our family of five from Lawrence, Kansas, to Miami, Florida, in a 1953 Ford. That was before they started building cars the size of houseboats. The back seat was never big enough for my older sister and brother, and me. Being the youngest, I got the middle. I remember repeatedly drawing lines with my finger in the fabric of the back seat on either side of me and telling my siblings not to cross either line. I tried to claim my territory, but it rarely worked. Eventually, after numerous complaints, "He touched me!" we got in trouble with dad.

Such is life. Most of our realms, given to us to rule, share borders with other people's realms. We can view this formation of boundaries as a challenge or a blessing. It can be a challenge if I see those whose realm borders mine as a potential threat. They might intrude on my control over my realm, similar to my brother or sister encroaching on my space in the back seat. However, it can be a blessing if we develop the type of relationship that makes them allies and team members.

Ruling in Community

One facet of the "radah" hypothesis that I have not discussed fully is that we were commanded as a race to rule. Adam needed a helper, and this need is extended to all of his descendants. We were never intended to rule alone. Much of the law of Moses, the wisdom literature in the Old Testament, the teachings of Jesus, and the epistles in the New Testament were written to teach us how to work together. Certainly, there are parts of my realm for which I and only I am responsible, but there are perhaps more parts of my realm for which I need the help of others. We need to leave behind the notion that ruling is being in control and realize that ruling is using my influence to bring order to the situation and then to fill it and the people involved with meaning and purpose. In fact, the level of influence I have is the measure of the border of my realm.

My realm consists of many smaller realms. That's because I have multiple relationships and responsibilities. So do you. Most of my responsibilities are shared with others. For instance, I teach at a Christian college. Our mission is to prepare students in a Bible centered environment for effective Christian life, service, and leadership. I cannot accomplish this mission by myself. I share this responsibility with all of the faculty, staff, and administration.

The problem with shared responsibility is getting everyone headed in the right direction. That begs the question, "What is the "right" direction?" Each person involved has a different perspective of what is the right direction. With limited information, they may each be assuming a different diagnosis of the problem. At the beginning of working together, each person is also only aware of their own capabilities and resources. This tunnel vision gives each person on the team a bias towards a strategy based only on their own capabilities and resources. Dr. Bruce Tuckman, a psychology professor, developed a theory

Rule in Harmony With Others

about the process each successful team must complete. He identified four stages of teambuilding: form, storm, norm, and perform. First, the people engaged in the task must form around common goals. As they begin to share their strategies to achieve their common goals, conflict develops from competing proposals. Tuckman called this the "storm" stage. Some teams are unsuccessful in overcoming this stage, dissolve the team, and as a result, fail to achieve their goals. If the team members can listen to and value each other's perspectives, they will discover more capabilities and resources within the team than they initially thought. As they learn about each other, they begin to accept normal roles on the team based on their unique capabilities. Each team member does the part that they are good at and trusts the other team members to do what they are good at. That is when the team starts performing effectively to accomplish their goals.[97]

The ability to listen to and value other's perspectives requires significant humility and emotional maturity. If I still needed constant affirmation of my worthiness, any suggestion that I am inadequate to address a situation or that my perspective is incomplete would make me feel attacked. That's when I would probably become defensive and fail to take advantage of the help others are trying to give me.

Ruling by Subduing

Genesis 1:28 reads, "God blessed them and said to them, "Be fruitful and increase in number; fill the earth and subdue it. Rule over the fish in the sea and the birds in the sky and over every living creature that moves on the ground." Not only were Adam and Eve to produce future generations, they were also to "fill the earth and subdue it." Filling the earth obviously includes increasing the human population. I think

---

97 Tuckman, Bruce W (1965). "Developmental sequence in small groups". Psychological Bulletin. 63 (6): 384–399.

we have pretty much succeeded at that. According to the "radah" hypothesis, "to fill" also meant to fill with meaning, purpose, and value. This type of filling often requires physically changing a thing to a form that has more meaning, purpose, and value for its ultimate purpose of glorifying God.

To make this change requires we subdue whatever we are filling. To "subdue" means to force your will upon something. Of course, our authority to "subdue" is limited to subduing the things within the realm God has given us. Genesis 1:11 reveals that the earth is designed to "produce vegetation: seed-bearing plants and trees on the land that bear fruit with seed in it, according to their various kinds." So our authority to force our will is limited to the earth, the plants, and the animals. Initially, this meant sowing and harvesting, and the domestication of animals.

However, our authority to subdue is also limited by ownership. In the story of Ruth, when Boaz wanted to buy Elimelek's land so he could marry Ruth, the author of the book inserted an explanation of the custom involved with the transfer of ownership. Ruth 4:7 reads, "Now in earlier times in Israel, for the redemption and transfer of property to become final, one party took off his sandal and gave it to the other. This was the method of legalizing transactions in Israel." To give the new owner the previous owner's sandal was a symbolic gesture that meant the buyer now has the right to walk on this property. By the way, the Hebrew word, kabash, translated in Genesis 1:28 "to subdue," is also translated "to tread on" (Micah 7:19 NIV) and "to trample." (Zechariah 9:15, NASB).

Walking the land was how it was subdued. The farmer walked the property to find and remove stones or anything else that would hinder a crop from growing. The farmer then walked the property to sow the seed. The farmer continued walking the property to observe the progress of the crop, remove weeds if wise, and guard it against thieves. Finally, when the crop was ripe, the farmer would walk the field to harvest the grain. The farmer subdued the land by walking on it, which enabled him to fill the field with meaning and purpose: to feed his family.

Today's concept of ownership is much more complicated. Of course, we have our own legal systems of deeding property to new buyers, but who owns a problem that everyone agrees needs to be resolved, or who owns a vision of what could be done in the future? Different cultures often have different rules for determining the authority to subdue. Modern cultures have legal property rights, copyrights, and privacy rights, etc. Organizations have bi-laws that define governing authority. In some cultures, the village elders must give approval before anything is significantly changed. In other cultures, the patriarch or matriarch rules "the roost" as long as they live.

Sorting out who has the authority to rule over a realm, whether that realm is a piece of property or the leadership role to lead an organization, is not always easy. I own a piece of property in Haviland, Kansas, but the local utility company dug a huge hole in my yard without even asking. Legally, they have the right to because my deed came with certain utility easements. So I own the property…sort of. The same is true in many organizations. One person may have the title of C.E.O, but everyone in the organization tends to seek someone else's opinion before they jump on board with the new direction.

In our home, we have defined realms of responsibility that come with a certain level of authority. Generally, anything that is outside the house or needs to be taken outside (e.g., the trash) belongs to one of my realms of responsibility. Inside the house is another matter. I keep our bank account balanced and do our taxes. My wife does the house cleaning, laundry, and we share the cooking and dishes (although I admit not entirely equally). On other matters, we need to talk because it is unclear who will take ownership of the issue.

Our realms are not just a list of tasks to be done. I might complete the tasks on my list but not fulfill the need. The tasks on my list may all be necessary, but insufficient to meet the need. Our realms are responsibilities to fulfill the need, whatever it takes. They also come with authority to do them how we think they should be done. For instance, I don't tell my wife how she should do the laundry. It is true that good communication is vital to a healthy marriage and every other important relationship. An essential part of that communication is the establishment of boundaries. Differences of opinion on in whose realm a responsibility lies can create conflict or an opportunity to create order in the relationship. Sometimes, through constructive conversation expectations of desired outcomes and the responsibility to achieve them can be clarified.

For instance, if I criticized my wife's way of doing my laundry, she could either accept my advice, explain to me why her way is better, or if we still disagree, she may suggest that I can do my own laundry however I would like. Which ever boundary we choose (her doing it her way, her doing it my way, or me doing it my way), establishing this boundary will create order in our relationship so that we can get back to filling each other. The bottom line is that subduing in a realm requires the authority of ownership—who is going to be responsible for bringing about the desired outcome. Sensitivity to ownership, levels of authority, and the boundaries of realms are at the heart of loving thy neighbor ruler.

Subduing My Sinful Desires and the Enemy

To the Jews who had believed Him, Jesus said, "If you hold to my teaching, you are really my disciples. Then you will know the truth, and

Rule in Harmony With Others

the truth will set you free" (John 8:31-32). The opposite is also true: When we exchange the truth about God for a lie, we wind up serving created things rather than the Creator (Romans 1:25). Either way, we can serve God, or we can serve the enemy. The issue is what we choose to believe. The spiritual battle we are called to fight is a battle over the truth, and the battleground is our minds. Of Satan, Jesus said, "When he lies, he speaks his native language, for he is a liar and the father of lies (John 8:44). James encouraged believers to "Submit yourselves, then, to God. Resist the devil, and he will flee from you" (James 4:7). As God-like rulers, we are called to separate the truth from the lies. This is how we subdue the enemy—both within and without. To do this requires more than just believing the right things. It also means being separate from the lies, in other words, incorporating the truth in our desires and behavior so that we demonstrate the truth. Jesus said, "I am the way, the truth, and the life." He did not say, "I have the truth," or "I can show you the truth." He said, "I am the truth." Following Jesus means not only believing and speaking the truth but also living the truth.

When Jesus said, "If you hold to my teaching," He meant more than getting our theology right. The word translated "hold to" ($\mu\varepsilon\acute{\iota}\nu\eta\tau\varepsilon$) is also translated "continue in" and "abide in." One of our human frailties is the tendency to be influenced by a half-truths. The enemy's lies always include a fair amount of truth—just enough to be believable. Otherwise, they would fool no one. To "hold to," "continue in," or "abide in" Jesus' teaching means to have His Word "at the ready" to fend off the enemy's lies. That is how Jesus resisted the devil's temptations in the wilderness. He quoted scripture as His defense against Satan's attacks. It reveals the value of memorizing scripture for securing our obedience when experiencing our own temptations. God's Word clears the fog and makes separating the truth from the lie easier to see.

In their epistles, both James and Peter encouraged the readers to "resist the devil" (James 4:7, 1 Peter 5:9). However, in both contexts, the precursor to successfully resisting the lies of the devil is humbly submitting to God. 1 Peter 5:6-8 reads,

> Humble yourselves, therefore, under God's mighty hand, that he may lift you up in due time. Cast all your anxiety on him because he cares for you. Be alert and of sober mind. Your enemy the devil prowls around like a roaring lion looking for someone to devour.

As long as we are confident in our own goodness, not willing to admit our absolute dependence upon God, we are simply a feast for the "roaring lion."

Ruling by Filling

I am constantly amazed that God works through us to accomplish His purposes. N.T. Wright observed,

> God made humans so that he could look after his world through this particular creature…That is one part of what it means to be in the image of God. God is not an object in the world, but he wanted from the first to be present and active in his world, so he created humans to be the means and mode of that presence and activity.[98]

Paul wrote in Ephesians 1:22-23, "And God placed all things under his feet and appointed him to be head over everything for the church, which is his body, the fullness of him who fills everything in every way." Jesus fills everything. In other words, He is in the process of ascribing to us a new meaning as the Bride of Christ. He is also assigning us an additional new purpose: to tell the new story of God's grace.

---

98 N.T. Wright (1989). Simply Good News, Why the gospel is news and what makes it good. New York: HarperCollins Publishers. pp. 97-98.

Rule in Harmony With Others

God's grace was not revealed until after Adam's sin, and the need for redemption arose (Gen 3). Now, through the work of God, we are being transformed "to the praise of his glorious grace, which he has freely given us in the One he loves" (Ephesians 1:6). In doing so, he is changing us from being "worthless" (Romans 3:12) to being "for the praise of his glory" (Ephesians 1:13). Which, as you may recall, is the ultimate purpose of creation (Psalm 19).

The goal of the enemy is just the opposite. His lies tell us that our struggles and accomplishments are meaningless, God's purpose is beyond our comprehension, and whatever we try to accomplish will be worthless in the end. He wants to empty us of all meaning, purpose, and value. But God has a strategy for how we might be filled to the "whole measure of the fullness of Christ." In Ephesians 4:11-13, Paul wrote,

> So Christ himself gave the apostles, the prophets, the evangelists, the pastors and teachers, to equip his people for works of service, so that the body of Christ may be built up until we all reach unity in the faith and in the knowledge of the Son of God and become mature, attaining to the whole measure of the fullness of Christ.

God provides church leaders to equip us for "works of service." We were never designed to be spectators. As N.T. Wright wrote, "He created humans to be the means and mode of [his] presence and activity."[99] The way we do that is by speaking the truth in love to one another. Speaking of how followers of Jesus mature and become equipped, Paul wrote,

> Then we will no longer be infants, tossed back and forth by the waves, and blown here and there by every wind of teaching

---

[99] N.T. Wright (1989). Simply Good News, Why the gospel is news and what makes it good. New York: HarperCollins Publishers. pp. 98.

and by the cunning and craftiness of people in their deceitful scheming. Instead, speaking the truth in love, we will grow to become in every respect the mature body of him who is the head, that is, Christ. From him the whole body, joined and held together by every supporting ligament, grows and builds itself up in love, as each part does its work. (Ephesians 4:14-16)

Speaking the truth in love might be with words or modeled as we live the truth. The truth to be communicated is clear: you have meaning by being part of the Body of Christ, you have purpose by being a God-like ruler over the realms God has given you, and you are valued to the full extent of the price Jesus paid to redeem you. Whatever type of ministry God has called you to and gifted you for, to be effective, it must be done out of love for others, having compassion for those who are living empty lives in a broken, chaotic world.

Rule in Harmony With Others

Discussion Questions

1. What are some of your shared responsibilities?

2. In your job, what "chaos" are you responsible for creating some kind of order? (Remember, chaos can be a type of brokenness that needs to be fixed, a natural and continuous need to be filled, or a potential yet to be realized.) How do you fill it with meaning and purpose in order to create value?

3. What memorized scriptures have helped you be obedient to Christ? What scripture will you memorize next?

4. Who do you know who is feeling empty? What could you say to them or do for them to help them know they mean a lot to you and that you see in them God working out His purposes through them?

11

Rule with Christ to Build the Kingdom of God

What will it take to bring the Kingdom of God to everyone? If the Kingdom of God is "the range of God's effective will," then It will take more than everyone becoming a Christian.[100] It will also require everyone to become God-like rulers who separate chaos into order and create value by filling things and other people with meaning and purpose. Only then will God receive the glory for which he created us. Can you imagine a world where everyone works together, each with their unique talents and skills, to create value? There would be no poverty, crime, or war. Everyone would focus on the realm they have been given to rule, staying within their boundaries to avoid causing conflict with their neighboring God-like ruler. They would be generating much more value than would be necessary to provide for their loved ones and everyone else.

Note that by "value," I mean much more than an increase in material goods or services. Value is the product of meaning and purpose. We value people and things to the extent that they are meaningful to us

---

100 John Ortberg (2018). Eternity is Now in Session. Carol Stream, IL: Tyndale House Publishers. pp. 20-21.

and help us accomplish our purposes. As we rule like God in our relationships, we add value to people by conveying meaning and purpose to them. Not only will they be more valuable to the community, but as they become more meaningful to us, we will personally value them more, loving them as God loves them. As we rule like God in our work related responsibilities, we add value to the company or organization and its products and services. Meaning and purpose are the foundation for motivation to achieve excellence. Trust and love relationships grow as we engage in the dance of building each other up. This is the abundant life Jesus calls us to (John 10:10).

This means that discipleship will be teaching them to "follow all that I commanded you" (Matthew 28:20), including how to separate and fill as God does. In this book, I have barely scratched the surface of what it means to glorify God with our whole lives and not just Sunday mornings. To suggest just a beginning list of the practical implications of God-like ruling, I will call on my particular faith heritage. Although I am sure from your faith heritage and others, we could create additional lists of equally valid implications of how to live out our faith.

My father traced our ancestry on his father's side back to 1682. On October 27th of that year, Miriam Short (who later married William White) stepped off the ship at the end of the same voyage that carried William Penn to establish the Quaker colony, Pennsylvania. She, William White, and their descendants have been Quakers through to my generation. The Quakers, especially the first few generations, led thousands to Christ and attempted to change their culture. Fair pricing of retailed goods instead of bartering, prison reform, and some of the concepts in our constitution came from the Quakers.

Some of their countercultural values can be listed by the first letter of each word, which spells S.P.I.C.E. (Simplicity, Peace, Integrity, Community, and Equality). I am certainly not saying that the concept of God-like ruling was understood by the early Quakers, but it is possible that their influence led me to seek a holistic perspective of my faith. The following are some brief examples of living as God-like rulers.

Simplicity: Manage your resources to love others as Jesus would

When someone begins to rule over their realms in the physical world (e.g., their home, their job, their community, etc.), they will naturally increase the value of their assets. Then, one faces the question of how to rule over their prosperity. God-like ruling over our wealth would imply separating between the funds needed for living and the funds available to share with others. In Luke 12:15-21, Jesus talked about a man in this situation,

> But He said to them, "Beware, and be on your guard against every form of greed; for not even when one is affluent does his life consist of his possessions." And He told them a parable, saying, "The land of a rich man was very productive. And he began thinking to himself, saying, 'What shall I do, since I have no place to store my crops?' And he said, 'This is what I will do: I will tear down my barns and build larger ones, and I will store all my grain and my goods there. And I will say to myself, "You have many goods stored up for many years to come; relax, eat, drink, and enjoy yourself!"' But God said to him, "You fool! This very night your soul is demanded of you; and as for all that you have prepared, who will own it now?' Such is the one who stores up treasure for himself, and is not rich in relation to God."

The man had more than he knew what to do with. Instead of sharing his excess with others, he devised a plan to keep it all to himself. God's rebuke of the man was not that he had no right to keep it all but that he lost a great opportunity to trade some of it for eternal reward. He could not buy his salvation, but he could invest it in the Kingdom of God by faith, anticipating a reward at the Judgment Seat of Christ (1 Corinthians 3:10-15, 2 Corinthians 5:10). Living simply means, in part, intentionally living below your means so that you will have money to share with those who are spreading the gospel and caring for the needy. By the way, the motivation for seeking rewards in heaven is not selfish. It is storing up treasures so that you may lay them at the feet of the King of Kings. You wouldn't want to arrive empty handed, would you?

Living simply also means separating between what is and is not needed. To the early Quakers, this meant, for instance, dressing and speaking simply. They did not follow the current fashions of dress and adornment. To them, the purpose of clothing was simply to cover the body and to protect it. They were too consumed by traveling to preach the gospel, caring for the needy and those in prison to have money for the latest fashions. It was their singular focus of bringing the Kingdom to their communities that kept life simple.

At that time, the English language was changing. People were no longer using the singular pronouns "thou, thee, and thine" to refer to an individual and instead were using the plurals "you and yours" as a means of flattery. Since Quakers spoke only the truth or what they believed to be true, they refused to grant all forms of flattery to wealthy or powerful people. They would have nothing to do with the subtle backscratching that is profoundly dishonest. They treated everyone the same; rich, poor, or imprisoned.[101]

Simplicity relates not only to how we treat others but how we treat ourselves. Sometimes our calendars get so full that we would be too busy to help others when a need arises, even if we wanted to. Everyone

---

101 Walter Williams (1962). The Rich Heritage of Quakerism, The past speaks to the present. Grand Rapids, MI: Eermans Publishing. p. 80.

needs margin in their life. Richard Swenson, M.D. wrote, "Margin less is being asked to carry a load five pounds heavier than you can lift. Margin is a friend to carry half the burden. Margin less is not having the time to finish the book you're reading on stress. Margin is having the time to read it twice."[102] I have to admit it is easy for me to over-commit myself. Sometimes this comes from a sincere desire to help fill the needs of my college or church. Other times, it results from a lack of perspective of what I am already doing and my need for margin in my life. There is a huge difference between being busy and being effective. It takes some wisdom and reflection to sort out the difference.

Richard Foster, in his book "Freedom of Simplicity," notes that the first step toward simplicity is the decision to seek first God's Kingdom.[103] It is that single focus that simplifies many of life's decisions. When I married my wife, I was seeking to become one with her in every area of our lives. For one thing, it clarified my priorities and many decisions. I separated myself from giving time to other people and things so I could pursue the goal of oneness with her. In Philippians 3:13, Paul wrote, "This one thing I do." The modern translation of which is often, "These forty things I dabble in." Basically, living simply is creating order in your life by separating between the essential and nonessential keeping your focus on the primary goal: God-like ruling for the glory of God.

Peace: Rule in Harmony with Others

God-like ruling requires staying within the boundary of the realm God has given you. We promote peace when we focus on taking care of our

---

[102] Richard Swenson (1992). Margin, Restoring emotional, physical, financial, and time reserves to overloaded lives. Colorado Springs, CO: NavPress. p. 13.
[103] Richard Foster (1981). Freedom of Simplicity. San Francisco: Harper & Row Publishers. p. 104

responsibilities rather than meddling in the responsibilities of others. This sometimes requires both patience and humility, but we are to grant others the respect and trust they deserve if God has given the particular realm to them and not us. It is easy at times to forget the sovereignty of God over our realms. It can be tempting to try political maneuvers to try to get our way concerning someone else's realm, but it usually results in conflict instead of peace.

To rule in harmony with others also means celebrating the strengths of others and leveraging your combined strengths to accomplish your purposes. Of course, to celebrate the strengths of others, you must first know what their strengths are. That is why relationship building is so important. To leverage each other's strengths, you need a trust relationship. To allow you to help me, I need to trust that you are competent to do your part of the process and that your goal is the same as mine. Each time we accomplish a task together, it strengthens our trust in each other, which will tend to make future conflicts less likely. We naturally communicate more with the people we trust, and more communication often reduces the risk of conflict due to misunderstandings.

Quakers thought about peace at three different levels. First, peace is an absence of inner conflict arising from the uncertainty of what to do or believe. These inner conflicts are sometimes the result of a lack of investigation into the facts of the issue or a lack of seeking God's direction. They can also be the result of not trusting God's timing, trying to make a decision before God makes the path clear.

Second, peace is an absence of conflict with others. It is assumed that if everyone follows God's direction, God will lead us together in harmony. Knowing that not everyone is following God, Paul wrote, "If possible, so far as it depends on you, be at peace with all people" (Romans 12:18). Paul's caveat, "so far as it depends on you," places on us the responsibility to avoid conflict in the first place and then to be at peace with others even when they are not in peace with us. This requires great faith in God, our defender, who will accomplish His purposes despite the opposition.

Third, peace is a sense of order and security. When things are in order, there is clarity on their meaning and purpose, thus alleviating uncertainty. When places and processes are orderly, it builds confidence that they have been thoughtfully designed to achieve their purposes. This confidence gives us peace that their purposes will be accomplished. When places and processes are secure, it means that care has been taken to keep them from harm. Again, this gives us peace of mind that their purposes will eventually be achieved.[104] In summary, peace is attained by God-like ruling over our realms and trusting God to redeem others to rule over their realms.

Integrity: Subdue Chaos

I loath buying used cars. It means that I have to prepare to first, inspect the car to make sure there aren't any hidden problems and second, enter the negotiating game to get a fair deal. One reason why we normally don't have to do this at the weekly market is because of the Quakers. In the 1600s, when someone went to the market, quality was suspect, and every purchase required negotiation skills. Buyer beware! But the Quakers determined to be truthful in word and deed. So the Quaker merchants were known for the quality of their goods, and they were the first to establish a non-negotiable "fair price" for their products. Soon, the Quaker merchants were getting the lion's share of the business. Their success led to a cultural shift in merchandising in

---

104 Glenn Leppert and David Kingrey (2020). The Heart of Friends, Quaker history and beliefs. Haviland, KS: Barclay College Publishers. p. 163.

Britain and her colonies. Even today, the name "Quaker" is appropriated in brand names such as "Quaker Oats" and "Quaker Oil" to imply quality and value.

When God first created the heavens and the earth, the earth was formless and empty. God had a plan, but the earth, in its chaotic state, did not yet meet the criteria of God's vision. But God had the will and the capability to subdue the chaos so that in six days, God's creation was all He intended it to be. Integrity is the character and competency to take things or situations that hold great potential and form them to fulfill their purpose. Even when there were setbacks such as Adam's sin, Israel's rejection of God as their King, and their repeated idolatry, God continued to work, shaping them through redemption to be the God-like rulers He envisioned. Integrity continues to work until the thing or situation meets the criteria required to fulfill its purpose.

Integrity is more than making responsible choices when a problem surfaces. It isn't just fixing things when they break. Integrity fixes the problem, of course, but also works to fix the system that allowed the problem to occur.[105] When something breaks down, generally, there are a variety of causes. Through wisdom and understanding of the system involved, many of those causes can be predicted and prevented. Integrity counts the cost of preventing chaos. The airlines regularly inspect their planes and replace parts before they wear out or break. They don't want to wait until an important part breaks while the plane is at 30,000 feet. They pay the cost of preventing the chaos of a plane crash before they take off.

You have no doubt bought something with "some assembly required." Did you ever notice that certain parts were designed so that they could only fit together the right way? That is called designing

---

105 W. Edwards Deming, (1988). Out of the Crisis, Cambridge, MA: MIT Center for Advanced Engineering Studies.

in quality, or the Japanese term for it: Poka-Yoke. Shigeo Shingo, an industrial engineer at Toyota, developed the concept of poka-yoke. It enabled Toyota to become the standard of quality in the automotive industry. Poka-Yoke ensures that the right conditions exist before a process step is executed, and thus preventing defects from occurring in the first place.[106] That's integrity!

Community: Fill Others with Meaning and Purpose

There were many times when Jesus spoke to the crowds (e.g., the sermon on the mount, Matthew 5-7) and the religious leaders (e.g., John 9:13-10:21), but most of His ministry years were spent with the disciples. There came a time when Jesus' mother and brothers asked to see him. Jesus used the opportunity to point out the bond that had developed between Him and His disciples. Jesus asked, "Who is my mother, and who are my brothers?" Pointing to His disciples, He said, "Here are my mother and my brothers. For whoever does the will of my Father in heaven is my brother and sister and mother" (Matthew 12:48-50). Through His investment in the disciples and their obedience to Him, they had developed a sense of community. Community is an awareness of belonging and endearment. Pointing at His disciples, Jesus affirmed them as His disciples and compared their meaning to Him with the typical bond between son and mother and between brothers.

My wife and I lead what we call "lab church" in our home on Sunday nights. It is designed to be a house church experience for the students during their four years in college. The attendees are Bible college students, and our focus is training them on how to do ministry. I tell them that the difference between a small group and a church is

---

106 Kanbanize.com. Accessed 9/20/21 from: https://kanbanize.com/lean-management/improvement/what-is-poka-yoke, n.d.

that people in a small group minister to each other, but a church has a mission outside itself. The students are each involved with different ministries. Some help with community or church youth programs, some write letters to prisoners or help with a recovery program, and others lead their own small group of students in a Bible study. We eat dinner together, discuss scriptures that relate to ministry, and then pray for each other's effectiveness in their ministry. In the process, we are building community.

Making disciples requires filling them with meaning and purpose, and that is best done by being in a relationship. It is the investment of time and attention in them that communicates, "You mean something to me, and to the Kingdom." Walking with them through their dry spells and fruitful harvests gives us many opportunities to affirm their purpose in the Kingdom by helping them discover their spiritual gifts, passions, and calling.

However, building a community is more than developing good feelings between people. You can be in community with people you don't particularly like. What binds the community together is having a common purpose. If we are making disciples, we are teaching them to obey all that Jesus has commanded us. If they are not committed to following Jesus, then no matter how much you like them, there is a certain sense in which they are in a different community. Filling them with purpose is helping them to see that by following Jesus, they can fulfill their ultimate purpose: glorifying God.

Equality: Value Everyone and Their Potential in the Kingdom of God

God makes people different. People have various amounts of different talents, intelligence, and other myriad variables (e.g., eye color, height, body shape, skin color, etc.). From God's perspective, each one is perfect for their purpose, with one exception. They have all become

Rule with Christ to Build the Kingdom of God

sinners. In Romans 3:12, Paul quotes from Psalm 14, "All have turned away, they have together become worthless; there is no one who does good, not even one."

However worthless for glorifying God people became, He does not throw them away. God never "cancels" us. He is in the business of redemption because in His infinite wisdom and love, He sees the potential in us to be redeemed until we are "his body, the fullness of him who fills everything in every way" (Ephesians 1:23). This is the transforming work of God in us that produces the fruit of the Spirit (Galatians 5:22).

To say that we will one day become the "fullness of Him who fills everything in every way" is saying quite a lot. It means that God can take something worthless for His purpose and make it everything He ever wanted it to be. To be the "fullness of Him" means that we become the God-like rulers who bring Him the glory He so richly deserves. In turn, He "fills everything in every way" because He is the sole source of meaning and purpose in everything—every person, every species, every galaxy, every part of all creation.

The Quakers have a long history of valuing everyone, despite their circumstances, because of "that of God in them." In other words, everyone has intrinsic value because they are created in the image of God. This perspective led them to behave toward others quite differently than was common in 17th century England. First, they refused to bow and scrape to magistrates and other dignitaries who expected them to show the same reverence toward them as they would toward God. The Quakers believed that we all equally share in the image of God. This landed many of them in prison. Once there, they realized the plight of the lowest level of society, the prisoners. That is when they worked diligently and successfully for prison reform. Quakers are also known for their early work to abolish slavery, promote education, and support women's rights.[107]

The point is that people have intrinsically equal potential to become the "fullness of God." Though we begin life as broken sinners, incapable of fulfilling our purpose of glorifying God, we can be redeemed to become who He intended us to be. However, this is the work of God, not the government or anyone else. Government can not give value to us simply by a redistribution of wealth. That might produce equity (an alluring fantasy of equal results) but not intrinsic equality. Our value is not what we possess but our God-designed, God-given, and God-redeemable potential to produce value by God-like ruling for the glory of God.

Conclusion

The "radah" hypothesis begins with Psalm 19:1-4, in which we learn that God is bubbling with excitement to give a full accounting of something never before displayed: His glory. This wordless narrative is etched into His design of every part of creation, including you and me. In Genesis 1:26-28 we discovered that our part to play in this grand epic about God's glory is that we were to be God-like rulers over our environment. But after Adam's sin, we changed the meaning of ruling to dominating each other. To discover what God-like ruling is supposed to look like, I surveyed the creation story, Adam's pre-fall activities, the life and ministry of Jesus, and God's ruling over us in the story of redemption. In all of these events, God-like ruling involved first separating the chaos to create order and then filling that order with meaning and purpose, which creates value. Therefore, to achieve

---

107 Walter Williams (1962). The Rich Heritage of Quakerism. Eerdmans Publishers. p. 147-148.

our primary purpose of glorifying our Creator, we are to implement these processes in everything we do.

Interestingly, secular psychologists independently discovered that humans from all cultures tend to do these same things, often just for enjoyment. Our systems of sensation and perception separate or distinguish our sensations to form perceptions that enable us to order, or make sense of, our experience. Because God loves diversity, He made our personalities a little different. That means that we don't all prioritize the same types of order. This can sometimes make life challenging but beautiful if we learn to celebrate our differences. Finally, psychologists discovered that we are almost incapable of not assigning meaning to our experience. It is an automatic response. Whether or not the meanings we ascribe to events are accurate, we use them to measure our progress toward our goals and ultimately to find purpose in life. From a secular point of view, purpose is self-generated, but from a Biblical perspective, our purpose is given to us by God's command and supported by our design as form follows function.

Finally, in exploring the practical applications of being God-like rulers in a sin broken world, I envisioned that we are kings and queens in the Kingdom of God. We each have our own current realm of responsibility given to us by God but which changes as we listen and follow the Spirit. Sometimes our realm borders the realms of others. When this is the case it is wise to communicate to establish clarity on the boundary between the realms. Sometimes God calls us for a time to join in cooperation with others to achieve a common goal. Each contributor will have their own realm of responsibility toward achieving the desired outcome. Whatever our part, it will involve separating to create order and filling that order with meaning, a purpose to create value. These processes are part of the DNA of our economy, our relationships, and our ministries. In short, they impact every aspect of

Kings and Queens in the Kingdom of God

our lives and reveal how we can glorify God every day of the week and not just on Sundays.

So we have a choice. We can focus on building our own kingdom—our financial wealth and influence to rule over others, or we can focus on God-like ruling within the realms God has given us in order to build the Kingdom of God. Which will you choose?

Epilogue

Remember Patrick, the bored accountant, Susan, the empty nester, and Hank, the burnt-out pastor? Assuming they have read this book and sincerely desire to apply the concepts of God-like ruling in the realms God has given them, let's check in with them to see how they have changed.

Patrick asked his wife if she could handle the kids for a couple of hours on Saturday morning so he could take a walk in the country to reflect and pray. He wanted to clarify in his heart that he was focusing on the realms that God had given him. Upon reflection, he did not doubt that God had led him to his job. Of course, his marriage, his kids, the house, and the dog were also realms within his responsibility.

As Patrick prayed for wisdom to rule in his position as an accountant, several thoughts came to mind. First, he recognized that his responsibility at work was to gather data, analyze it, report his findings, and make recommendations. His boss had often asked him for his thoughts on upcoming decisions, but Patrick had tried to avoid making any projections for fear of being wrong. Second, he realized that he was only doing the minimum analysis necessary to get through each month. He wondered if "separating to create order" meant for him doing a long-range study to see if his company had gone through repeated financial cycles that would help him understand where they are now and what to anticipate in the future. Filled with a new passion for his "work" realm, he was looking forward to getting started on Monday to begin his research.

Third, he hadn't thought before about filling other people. He realized it had been way too long since he told his wife and kids what they meant to him. He asked God to help him understand his wife's needs that only a husband can fill. Also, as he thought of each of his kids, he realized how different they were from each other. He thought about what each child seemed to want constantly. Sarah often colors pictures or makes things with Legos and then asks, "What do you think?" looking for affirmation of a job well done. Kenny always wants to wrestle. Benny likes to be held, especially on walks outside. He decided to hire a babysitter to give his wife and him some uninterrupted time to discuss how they will fill their children with God's love and purpose.

Patrick's thoughts then turned to the people at work. He wasn't sure if any of them knew he was a Christian. He wanted to distinguish himself as a believer, but he didn't want to fill his office with "Christian trinkets." He decided he would begin by showing more interest in the people he worked with and for. That would give him opportunities to privately pray for them, and if God opens the right opportunity, to share his faith journey with some of them. If the research on financial cycles proves to be helpful, he might even tell his boss he was praying about how to do a better job, and that God gave him the idea.

* * *

Susan got up the next morning, still thinking about how she could do God-like ruling. One of her friends had told her that even though

Epilogue

their son was now married, parenting never really ends. That made her worry about becoming the dreaded nosey mother-in-law. No, she needed to redraw the boundaries in her relationship with her son. She knew that God's plan was for a man to leave his father and mother and to "cleave" to his wife. Susan committed to praying for their son and his wife and then trying her best to save her advice for whenever they asked for it. Besides, it would be much more fulfilling to see her son and daughter-in-law work through their challenges together as they seek to follow God in their own way. Affirming this type of "separating to create order" in her relationship with her son and his wife was not easy. She knew she would need God's help to stay within her new realm of mother-in-law.

Susan turned her attention to her online business. By 11:00 in the morning, she had responded to all of her customers and suppliers. There was not much more she could do at that point. Besides, the income she got from the business was just her "fun money." She checked her company's bank balance and realized she had more than enough for a little vacation. A half-hour later, having scrolled through several ads for destination resorts, she doubted a weekend here or there would fill her emptiness. She checked her e-mail one more time and saw one from their church. It asked for prayer for a homeless shelter downtown that needed volunteers.

Susan was about to say a quick prayer for the shelter when a thought came to her. Why not swing down by the shelter to find out more about it? She needed to get out of the house anyway.

Rounding the corner where the shelter was located, she was surprised to see a line of people, mostly women and children, waiting outside. The shelter wasn't open yet for lunch, and it was already 1:00. She drove up the alley behind the shelter, parked her car, and knocked on the back door. An elderly lady beamed at her and said, "Oh, thanks for coming! Here's an apron. We're just about ready to open and start serving. The trays are over there. Jasmine will show you how we do things around here."

Susan, somewhat shocked to find herself "volunteered," put on the apron and headed for the stack of serving trays. Looking around, she saw stacks of sandwiches on a center island and another lady putting sandwiches on plates.

"Bless you, sister, for helping out today," Jasmine said. "You can see we are short-handed. My name is Jasmine; what's yours?"

"Susan, but I…"

"That's ok, honey, you'll catch on. Now, here are some gloves, put two plates and two sets of silverware, and …."

By 2:30, they had fed the last person in line. Susan was tired but was amazed at how much she enjoyed serving these people. She even got the chance to hold a baby while his mother tended to her two other children. Susan discovered that they came most days for lunch and then came back in the evening. She listened to the mom, Charelle, tell her story of becoming homeless and how grateful she was for the help with the baby. Realizing that she had made a difference by holding a baby for a few minutes made her see how fulfilling this work is. Returning to the kitchen, Susan found Jasmine and the other lady wiping down the counters.

"So, what'd you think?" asked Jasmine with a big smile.

"It was amazing. I'm surprised that I enjoyed it so much!"

"Really? Why?" Jasmine asks.

"Well… I've never interacted with…"

"The homeless? Yeah, they are just people with real problems."

"Do they ever…?" Susan hedges, not wishing to ask anything offensive.

Epilogue

"Get off the street? Some do. We have a mentor program to help them with life skills. The ones who go through that program are the most likely to."

"Wow, that sounds exciting!"

"We are having a training program for mentors that will start in a few weeks. Would you be interested in that?" Jasmine asks with a big smile on her face.

"I think I might be. Let me pray about it."

That evening, Susan animatedly shared her experience with her husband. He was surprised to see her so excited but thanked God that she was finding a new purpose. After they talked about his concerns for her safety, they prayed together for God's leading.

A year later, Susan could hardly believe how far Charelle had come. She had completed the life skills program, found a job and an apartment. Susan and Charelle had become more than just mentor and mentoree; they had become friends and prayer partners. At her graduation from the life skills program, Charelle shared how much it meant to her to have a mentor who really cared. She testified that she no longer felt like trash and knew God had plans for her and her children.

* * *

Pastor Hank put down this book and whispered, "Lord, help me." He picked up his Bible and turned again to Ephesians 4:11-13,

> So Christ himself gave the apostles, the prophets, the evangelists, the pastors and teachers, to equip his people for works of service, so that the body of Christ may be built up until we all reach unity in the faith and in the knowledge of the Son of God and become mature, attaining to the whole measure of the fullness of Christ.

It struck him that the one thing he was called to do (equip his people for works of service), he wasn't doing. He had gotten into the trap of just doing everything himself because it was faster, easier, and frankly helped him keep things going the way he wanted. Hank wondered if he started delegating some of the administrative tasks, the board might think he was shirking his duties. Apparently, they too had come to believe that's why they paid him.

Hank got up from his desk to get away from the in-basket and telephone, stopped for a cup of coffee, and drove to a local park. He opened his journal and started listing the repeated tasks he wanted to separate from himself. Then he categorized the tasks into a couple of jobs that could be handled better by a volunteer who is gifted in administration. These new ministry job descriptions then led him to think of people in his congregation who might be interested in taking them on.

At the next board meeting, Hank explained how his new insight into ruling like God rules led him to create some possible ministry opportunities for others. After the board discussed how they would ensure that the tasks got done consistently and correctly, they approved.

"So, Hank, what are you going to do with all your extra time?" asked one board member.

"I'm glad you asked. First, it will take some time to recruit and train each volunteer. Then once I have them going, I'll just have to touch base with them monthly to see what's getting done. That is unless one of you would be willing to supervise them."

"You know, supervising people is what I do," said one board member. "If you include me in the training, I could take that responsibility."

"Great. I'll call you after the Lord provides a volunteer, and we'll set up some training times. Beyond that, I've been thinking about all the things I haven't had time for… especially prayer. I'm concerned

Epilogue

that we are adding ministries to our church because we see the need but aren't making sure that we are the ones called to meet that need."

"If we don't start a recovery program, then who will?"

"I don't know, but I think God gives each of us a realm to rule and that might apply to churches as well. By ruling, I mean creating order and then filling people with God's meaning and purpose for their life. A recovery ministry might, or might not, be within the realm God is giving us. We need to seek God's direction on this."

"Are you saying God might be calling another church in town to start a recovery program?"

"We need to separate ourselves, in other words, "sanctify ourselves" for the ministry God has for this church. This means not allowing every need in the community to distract us from what God is calling us to do. Before we talk any more about a recovery ministry, let's each invest some time to pray about it and ask for God's direction one way or the other."

The board agreed, and they dismissed the meeting in prayer before 10:00 pm for the first time in recent memory.

A year later, Hank is enjoying the third night this week at home with his wife. He was delighted that he had time to be more supportive of Jill's ministry and her need to care for her mother. When he joined Jill at the kitchen table, she mentioned,

"I heard from my friend Meghan that the big church on the other end of town has developed a very successful recovery program. I guess they have several gifted counselors in their congregation."

"That's what I've heard too. I'm really glad for them; they are doing important work for the Kingdom."

"You know, Hank, if our church had tried that, we wouldn't have had the resources for the ministry to foster parents that has been a huge blessing to those families."

Kings and Queens in the Kingdom of God

"And our church as well! All those kids in our children's program have certainly livened things up. I never knew we had so many people interested in ministering to kids."

The three scenarios written in this book are completely fictitious; however, I hope that they help illustrate the possible impact of God-like ruling on our daily lives. In the appendices you will find practical helps for finding the borders of your realm and for God-like ruling in a particular situation.

If you would like to have Keith to come speak at your church or lead a small group workshop, please feel free to contact him at: keith.white@barclaycollege.edu.

Appendix A

Coaching Questions to Help You Discover Your Realm

A coaching question is an open-ended question designed to inspire you to think and pray about the answer. Usually, there is no one right answer. There can be wrong answers. A wrong answer might be the result of not wanting to think about the topic right now, so you put down an answer based on your first thought or what someone has told you, or what everyone else is doing. Another wrong answer could be the result of rushing through the process to get to the bottom line without waiting for direction from God. Most believers don't hear audible messages from God. Still, after praying about the topic, thinking through multiple options and their implications, seeking God's wisdom, seeking the wisdom of godly believers, and waiting for God's answer, you will either:

1. Get a sense of peace in your spirit that one or more answers follow God's leading, or
2. Get a lack of peace over the whole issue. This general lack of peace probably means God has an option that you have not yet considered.

Coaching Questions

The list of questions below will begin with the seven areas of every believer's realm. Following these questions will be some questions relating to other possible areas within your realm. I suggest you begin a journal of your thoughts, prayers, and research on each question so that at the end, you can review the process and your answers.

1. **My Heart** (Proverbs 4:23, Matthew 15:1-20, Matthew 22:37, 2 Corinthians 4:16, Ephesians 1:18, Philippians 4:6-7, Colossians 3:1-17, 2 Timothy 2:22, Hebrews 3:7-19, James 4:8, 1 John 3:19-22)

    a. Review the scriptures listed above and note any questions you have about their meaning to the original readers. What resources will you use to find the correct interpretation of each passage? (There are several good resources online, such as Biblegateway.com, Biblehub.com, and preceptaustin.org, etc.)

    b. Which passages challenged or convicted you the most? In what way?

    c. How would you briefly describe your general attitude toward God? How would your attitude toward God compare to your attitude toward your lover or best friend?

    d. What does your spending time with God look like? How could it be more meaningful?

    e. What sins do you repeatedly confess (1 John 1:9) and are struggling to subdue?

    f. What gives you the greatest joy in your relationship with God?

2. **My Relationships** (Romans 12:9-21, 1 Corinthians 13, Ephesians 5:21-6:9, Philippians 2:1-11)

    a. Review the scriptures listed above and note any questions you have about their meaning to the original readers. What resources will you use to find the correct interpretation of each passage? (There are several good resources online, such as Biblegateway.com, Biblehub.com, and preceptaustin.org, etc.)

b. Which passages challenged or convicted you the most? In what way?

c. List the names of only your significant relationships and the category they belong in, such as a spouse, relative, friend, co-worker, neighbor, mentor, mentee, pastor, teacher, classmate, etc.

d. Rank each relationship on a scale of 1 to 10 from your perspective on how comfortable your relationship is with them. (1 = extremely uncomfortable, 5 = just ok, 10 = extremely comfortable) Note: "comfort" in a relationship is mostly related to the level of trust you have with that person and whether they bring you energy or drain energy from you.

e. Rank each relationship on a scale of 1 to 10 from their perspective on how comfortable your relationship is with them. (1 = extremely uncomfortable, 5 = just ok, 10 = extremely comfortable) Note: "comfort" in a relationship is mostly related to the level of trust you have with that person and whether they bring you energy or drain energy from you.

f. What did you learn about your relationships from your list and how you scored their comfort level?

g. For those relationships that you scored from 1 to 4, what could you do to repair that relationship? (Romans 12:18 If it is possible, as far as it depends on you, live at peace with everyone.)

h. How could you improve how much or how little you should prioritize your time spent on each of these relationships in relation to the other relationships or other interests?

i. Name some people who were not on your list but who should be, or you'd like to have on your list of significant relationships. How could you develop those relationships?

3. **My Commitments** (Proverbs 16:1-3, Matthew 5:31-37, Colossians 3:22-24, James 4:13-17)

   a. Review the scriptures listed above and note any questions you have about their meaning to the original readers. What resources will you use to find the correct interpretation of each passage? (There are several good resources online, such as Biblegateway.com, Biblehub.com, and preceptaustin.org, etc.)

   b. Which passages challenged or convicted you the most? In what way?

   c. List each of your ongoing commitments, including the people who depend on you, such as a spouse, children, and others who need your assistance, your job(s), your memberships, your volunteer positions, etc.

   d. Would you say that you are over scheduled, or that you have time for new commitments? What time in your week is available for a new commitment apart from the margin we need in our schedule to be available for the unexpected?

   e. How could you improve how high or low you should prioritize your time spent on each of these commitments in relation to the other commitments?

   f. What commitments do you need with integrity "to work your way out of," why?

   g. What commitments do you need to make or raise your level of commitment? Why?

   h. Who could best give you an external perspective of your number of commitments and your level of commitment to the most important ones?

4. **My Health** (1 Corinthians 6:19, Ephesians 5:29, 1 Timothy 4:8, 3 John 1:2)

a. Review the scriptures listed above and note any questions you have about their meaning to the original readers. What resources will you use to find the correct interpretation of each passage? (There are several good resources online, such as Biblegateway.com, Biblehub.com, and preceptaustin.org, etc.)

b. Which passages challenged or convicted you the most? In what way?

c. How would you assess your overall health and fitness?

d. What behaviors to promote better health are you already consistently doing?

e. What habits to promote better health do you need to develop?

f. What habits to promote better health do you need to begin?

g. What metrics do you use to measure health trends? (e.g. weight, pulse, blood pressure)

h. Who could partner with you to help you be more successful in maintaining or improving your health?

5. **My Learning** (Proverbs 1:1-7, 1 Timothy 4:13-16, 2 Timothy 2:15)

a. Review the scriptures listed above and note any questions you have about their meaning to the original readers. What resources will you use to find the correct interpretation of each passage? (There are several good resources online, such as Biblegateway.com, Biblehub.com, and preceptaustin.org, etc.)

b. Which passages challenged or convicted you the most? In what way?

c. In what subject do you feel the greatest need to learn? Why?

d. What are you reading? How do you capture what you are reading into your long-term memory, or at least keep it in an accessible form of storage?

e. What other ways are you taking in new information? Are they effective for helping you learn what you want to learn?
   f. With whom do you process what you are learning? Are they helpful to you?
   g. What changes to your ruling over your realm are a result of what you have learned in the past year?

6. **My Career and Finances** (Matthew 6:19-34, Mark 12:13-17; 12:41-44; Luke 10:25-37, Romans 13:7-8)
   a. Review the scriptures listed above and note any questions you have about their meaning to the original readers. What resources will you use to find the correct interpretation of each passage? (There are several good resources online, such as Biblegateway.com, Biblehub.com, and preceptaustin.org, etc.)
   b. Which passages challenged or convicted you the most? In what way?

   Finances
   c. With whom do you need to communicate to and find consensus with when making financial decisions? How well is that process working now?
   d. If you have debts, what is your plan for getting out of debt?
   e. How do you feel about the percentage of your income that you give to the Lord? If you feel it is insufficient, then how would you plan to change it?
   f. What future additional expenses are in the next few years that you need to be saving for? What do you own that is wearing out and will need to be repaired, remodeled, or replaced?
   g. How could you simplify your life to reduce your cost of living?

h. How could you learn to be more successful in your financial planning?

Career

i. How would you assess you progress toward your career goals?

j. What do you need to learn in order to do a better job as a student, employee, owner, or retiree? What resources would provide that information and how could you access them?

k. Do you have a sense of peace from God that you are currently in the position, or working for the right company, where He wants you? How have you sought and received His direction on this?

l. If you do not have peace from God, then what is your plan to explore other alternatives?

m. Other than God, with whom do you need to consult with when making career decisions? Who would be affected by your making career changes?

n. Who could be a career mentor to you? Other than your boss, who has experience and wisdom about your current career or the career you aspire to?

o. What educational degrees or certifications will be required for the career you aspire to? What are your plans for carving out the time for this and for paying for it?

7. **My Witness** (1 Peter 3:15, 1 Corinthians 6:1-6, 1 Thessalonians 4:9-12, 1 Timothy 3:7, 2 Timothy 1:8)

   a. Review the scriptures listed above and note any questions you have about their meaning to the original readers. What resources will you use to find the correct interpretation of each passage? (There are several good resources online, such as Biblegateway.com, Biblehub.com, and preceptaustin.org, etc.)

b. Which passages challenged or convicted you the most? In what way?

c. Who is watching you to learn from you how Christians talk and behave?

d. With whom are you cultivating a relationship in order to help them find their way back to God?

e. With whom are you cultivating a relationship in order to help them grow in their relationship with Christ or the effectiveness of their ministry?

f. How do you minister to others? Note: I define ministry as using your spiritual gift to love others and through that expression of love (whether preaching, leading a Sunday school class or small group, cleaning church bathrooms, giving, balancing the churches financial books, or writing a note of encouragement) helps them to sense God's order and the fullness of His love.

g. Who could best give you an external perspective of your Christian witness or ministry and how you might improve it?

Appendix B

A Guide for God-like Ruling in a Particular Situation

So, how do you actually do God-like ruling to find fulfillment and glorify God? In this appendix, I am proposing a pathway, a series of issues to think and pray through, to guide you through the process of creating order from chaos and filling it with meaning, purpose, and value. God-like ruling is a journey that has a beginning and several stops along the way before we finally experience fulfillment in the end by giving glory to God for all of it.

The "30,000" foot view of this pathway looks like this:

1. Examine the Chaos
2. Explore the Potential Meanings
3. Clarify the Purposes
4. Subdue the Chaos
5. Celebrate Created Value
6. Give Glory to God

Below, I will explain the need for each of these steps and give you several questions for you to consider as you seek God's wisdom for your situation. In essence, this is a thinking and praying journey. Both thinking and praying can be hard work. That is why we often don't do them as much as we should. The value of setting out on a long journey like this is weighed by the amount of pain in the chaos we are experiencing. That chaos could be a broken relationship or, on the positive side, an opportunity to create a significant new value.

Examine the Chaos

Every journey begins where you are. But, where exactly is that? Before Nehemiah started rebuilding Jerusalem, he took a midnight ride around the city to examine the brokenness of the walls. He wanted to see what he was up against before he proposed any solutions. The chaos in your particular situation may be hard to comprehend fully. In taking the time to understand the real problem(s) causing the chaos, you may make many "discoveries" that will influence how you prepare for your journey.

1. Pray for Wisdom and Insight: Always begin with a humble spirit that acknowledges that your understanding is limited and God's is

not. James 1:5 reveals that God generously gives wisdom to those who ask for it. Why would anyone not take Him up on His offer? In our pride and foolishness, we sometimes think, "I got this!" when in reality, we probably have no clue.

2. Give God Time to Lead You: The enemy often tells us to hurry up and do something, but God calls us to wait on Him. Jesus said, "My sheep hear my voice." As our Shepherd, He leads us if we are patient to listen instead of running ahead and possibly causing more problems.

3. Check Your Realm: The next question to ask yourself is whether this is your journey to take or is it for someone else? There may be a real need, but you may not be the one to lead the journey. You might be the needed team member or the "behind the scenes" prayer support. Or, this particular chaos may be distracting you from a different source of chaos on which God wants you to focus your God-like ruling efforts.

    a. Why do you think this chaos is your responsibility to order and fill?

    b. Is this a need for which God has prepared you through education or experience?

    c. Is this a need you believe God is leading you to fill?

    d. To what extent is this a current need in your own realm? Do you need to "remove the log in your own eye" before trying to help someone else?

    e. Is this the greatest source of chaos in your life? Or, at least the most important at this moment for you to bring glory to God through God-like ruling?

4. Analyze the Chaos: One of the greatest follies is trying to solve the wrong problem or setting the wrong goal. We naturally want to jump in and solve the problem as soon as possible because we

want to alleviate the pain. But this can lead us to make false assumptions based on limited information. Cooler heads take the time to observe the facts of the situation and stop themselves from just guessing what might be the problem.

a. What do you know for sure in this situation? What questions do you need to ask to get more information? Sir Francis Bacon wrote, "The significant question is the half of knowledge." Framing the right question(s) will help you focus on the real problem.

b. Who has already gone through a similar journey that might be able to help you see the problem with more clarity and depth of perspective? In our pride, we are tempted to try to solve our problems all by ourselves. We hesitate to ask for help. Wise travelers know the value of a guide and how their insights can shorten the journey and increase your success.

c. How is this chaos affecting the feelings of all who are impacted by it? Many times the greatest challenge is overcoming the emotional resistance to implementing solutions. That's because solutions require change, and change is scary. However, the emotions of others are within their realm. We are not responsible for their emotions, but being aware of them may be essential to your success.

d. What in this particular chaos breaks the heart of God? Remember, this is ultimately about bringing glory to God through God-like ruling. Whether addressing chaos caused by sin or addressing an opportunity to create new value, God longs to see His children tell their part of the story of His glory through the way He has designed us. Perhaps lost opportunity breaks His heart in some similar way as lost people.

Explore the Potential Meanings

When we rule like God rules, we transform the chaos around us from meaninglessness to meaningfulness. Things begin to make sense. Strategies begin to succeed. People begin to work in harmony toward complementary goals and grow in love for each other through their shared victories. That's the goal, but this part of the journey is still observing and learning about the impact of the chaos.

The first casualty of chaos is the truth. Chaos is what we feel when our experience does not match God's reality or when there is an opportunity to create new meaningfulness. The enemy pawns his lies to create the pain of chaos in our lives. Truth is also discarded by not believing in the possibility of a new, more meaningful way of living. True meaning is always possible if we follow the Spirit's leading and seek His truth to rule over our realm like God rules over His.

The second casualty of chaos is either broken personal relationships or the need to create new functional relationships. Personal relationships are broken by a lack of trust and appreciation for the other person. Functional relationships are the communication and physical processes needed to produce the desired outcome. Both types of relationships create meaning.

1. What would creating order in this situation mean for your realm? Your realm is who you are and all that God has given to you to rule. Every change creates implications of new possibilities. Every effort also has costs and benefits to consider before starting the journey. How would fulfilling this need or creating a new reality change who you are?

2. What would creating order in this situation mean to the realm of others? Almost everything we do affects other people in some way. Who are the people who would be impacted by the change in this situation? From their perspective, what costs and benefits

would they experience? Remember, God-like ruling is ruling over the situation, not over others. Therefore, we need to respect the boundaries of other's realms.
3. What would creating order in this situation mean to God? The ultimate goal is always that God be glorified by our God-like ruling. He is glorified when we love Him and others as ourselves. He is also glorified when our God-like ruling produces even greater value in our realms.
4. What functional relationships need to be created? Functional relationships allow things to work together. They are the communication pathways and the physical processes that produce the end product. How will you create new paths of communication between those who have information and those who need it? How will the physical process work? How will it start, develop, and finish? Who will manage it to keep it on track? How will you know if it is working?

Clarify the Purposes

We all have our own agendas. God-like ruling assumes being goal driven to restore brokenness and to create new types of order that will fulfill us. Having a sense of our purpose gives us hope for the future. Further, the purpose God gives you defines the borders of our realm. The problem with fallen God-like rulers is that we often create our own purposes rather than receiving them from God. We'd prefer to build our kingdom for our glory rather than God's kingdom for His glory. This tension will be present within any situation involving fallen God-like rulers. Being aware of the personal agendas involved will be essential to your success. One of life's greatest sources of fulfillment is finding a common purpose with others and helping each other succeed.
1. What possibilities could be realized by creating order and filling

the need in this situation? What is the ultimate goal? A vision or mission statement is helpful to clarify your purpose. It keeps you focused on what is important rather than getting entangled in things that won't help you achieve your purpose.
2. How will creating order in this situation affect the realms of others? Fulfillment happens when we create value. God-like ruling produces outcomes that we and others value because they help us achieve our purposes. How will the proposed change affect their self-image, their responsibilities, and the resources they need to rule over their realm?
3. How will creating order in this situation advance the Kingdom of God? The Kingdom of God is wherever believers are doing God's will. The Kingdom of God advances as more and more people find their way back to God and begin to serve Him. Every opportunity for God-like ruling holds the potential to be a witness to those outside the Kingdom of God that God's way is best. God-like ruling doesn't always involve evangelism, but it does advance the Kingdom of God because it is doing God's will.
4. How will God get the glory? According to Jonathan Edwards, God's ultimate purpose for creation is to reveal His glory. Our response to His unimaginable beauty should be to give him the glory He richly deserves. One way we do that is by being God-like rulers as He designed us to be. Giving testimony to how God prepared you, the wisdom and leading He provided, and the grace He gave you through the process is the least we can do.

Subdue the Chaos

Now that you have analyzed the situation and have determined it is within your realm of responsibility, it is time to do something about it. Subduing the chaos means doing whatever is within your authority to create order, meaning, purpose, and value in this situation. God-like ruling produces real and lasting change that fulfills the need and/or fills with potential. The following six actions to take are not necessarily sequential. Instead, they are the multiple things you will repeatedly be doing until the need is fulfilled.

1. **Seek God's Wisdom.** God-like ruling continually seeks the wisdom that He promises us in James 1:5 with the caveat that we believe that we will receive it. That means waiting in expectation until we hear from God. Believers experience God's direction in myriad ways. Listen for promptings and checks in your spirit. Once you have peace, step out in faith and do what He is leading you to do.
2. **Explore Possible Strategies.** Everyone has a comfort zone based on their personality. The danger is that we will select a strategy to fulfill the need that has more to do with our comfort zone than with what will be effective. Consider as many different possible strategies that you can think of and ask for the perspective of those more experienced in subduing this kind of chaos. Of course, your chosen strategy may need revising as you learn more about the situation.
3. **Separate the Truth from the Lie to Create Order.** The lie is almost always that the need can not be fulfilled or the brokenness cannot be restored. With God, all things are possible. (Matthew 19:26). When you invested time in examining the chaos, the goal was to identify the lie. Speak the truth to counter the lie. This could be anything from reaffirming God's word to your own situation, encouraging someone who is broken, making a scientific discovery that reveals God's intelligent design, teaching a child to read, or proposing a strategy to create new value. You have already established that fulfilling this need is within the realm God has given you. You have been prepared and called by God to subdue

this particular chaos. Now is the time to speak the truth in love so that we will,

> Grow to become in every respect the mature body of him who is the head, that is, Christ. From him the whole body, joined and held together by every supporting ligament, grows and builds itself up in love, as each part does its work. (Ephesians 4:15-16)

In the context of this passage, Paul is referring specifically to the church and Christ's redemptive work in us. However, the principles of growth to maturity, the headship of Christ, the interconnectedness of a loving community, and diverse roles and responsibilities all apply to God-like ruling.

4. **Create Meaning.** Building relationships creates meaning. Personal relationships develop through expressions of respect, trust, and love. Functional relationships develop through designed changes in the physical and informational environment. Creating meaning through relationships requires sensitivity toward the appropriate context and rate at which the relationship can be successfully built. God-like ruling also assumes that the meanings to be created are beyond what a fulfilled need means to me and include what it means to others.

5. **Achieve Purposes.** When God separated His creation to create order, He gave a unique purpose to each part. That is the essence of design. Purposes are owned by individuals but can be shared by communities. God-like ruling respects that everyone and every situation have a God-given purpose which we dare not presume to be in our realm. It is not for us to intrude into God's purpose in a situation to alleviate the chaos we perceive. God is at work, ruling over creation in ways of which we are unaware. However, God has given you a realm to rule. Within your realm, you have a purpose

– the restoration of God's order and the creation of new value. By achieving our God-given purposes, we are fulfilled.

6. **Manage the Journey to Fulfillment.** Every human activity needs to be managed. We live in flux and need to constantly adjust to changes that would affect the outcome. This journey is also a sequence of many individual actions that need to be implemented and assessed for their effectiveness. A critical element of management is to be clear about what is fulfillment in this situation for you and others. Only then will you know when you have fulfilled your purpose and brought glory to God.

Celebrate Created Value

God loves to celebrate and wants us to celebrate with Him. It is part of entering into His rest. He created feasts for the Israelites to celebrate their blessings, but perhaps the greatest celebration will be the marriage feast of the Lamb in heaven foretold in Revelation 19:1-10. It is during the celebration of newly created value that we get to experience the feeling of fulfillment. It is a sacred time to reflect on what God has enabled you to accomplish and honor all who helped you.

1. **Reflect on the Newly Created Value.** Take the time to compare the previous chaos and associated pain with the value of the new sense of order and harmony with God's plan for your realm. Consider the effort it required and the benefits it has produced. Let this reflection build your faith that God can work through you to subdue the next chaos by creating order, meaning, and achieving purposes to create value.
2. **Appreciate the Assistance You Received.** We all stand on the shoulders of others. Your fulfillment has come in part from a price paid by others. Celebrate their contribution by showing your appreciation and acknowledging their fulfillment in addition to yours.

3. **Rejoice over the Progress.** Joy is a fruit of the Spirit. (Galatians 5:22) In other words, joy is at the heart of God's will for you. Happiness is fleeting, but joy is steadfast and will sustain you through the next chaos. Joy is not something we can create. It is given to us by the Holy Spirit (1 Thessalonians 1:6). Our only responsibility is to receive it in its fulness.

Give Glory to God

The ultimate reason for our existence is to glorify the One who created us. A major theme of this book is that we can glorify God by what we do. But we also need to glorify Him by what we say.

1. **Praise God for Newly Created Value and its Implications.** As you begin to speak the truth to counter the lie causing the chaos, new value will begin to emerge. Praise God for each advance and the further possibilities it provides.
2. **Praise God for Working through Your Realm in this Situation.** God did not have to choose you. It is a privilege and honor when God calls us to participate with Him to subdue the chaos and create new value. Praise God for the opportunity to be used by Him.
3. **Praise God for the God-like Ruler He is Making You.** Every journey from chaos to value changes us. We are being molded and shaped by the experience. Praise God that He is creating meaning in your realm and achieving His purpose in you.
4. **Speak of His Wonderous Works to Others.** We all need to hear about how God is working. A testimony of what God has done reminds us that we cannot do God-like ruling without Him. Jesus said, "Apart from me you can do nothing" (John 15:5). Encourage others with your story of how God has enabled you in this journey.

Acknowledgments

Thank you to Paul White, my younger, smarter brother, and co-author of *The 5 Languages of Appreciation in the Workplace*, who encouraged me and opened doors for this book to be published. To Dr. Derek Brown, who gave valuable feedback on what was most beneficial. To Rachel Mortimer, who directed the editorial process and graciously refined the manuscript to be more precise, easier to read, and included more practical applications. Finally, to Debbie White, my new wife, who read every page and provided valuable insights from a reader's perspective.

About the Author

Keith White, Ph.D, is currently a college professor of 16 years and the Director of Institutional Effectiveness at Barclay College in Haviland, KS. He has a B.A. through Barclay College, a M.R.E. through Nazarene Theological Seminar, and a Ph.D. through the University of Kansas in Educational Psychology and Research. Keith has not only studied at various institutions but has put his studies to work as an Associate Pastor, a Pastor, and a church planter. He enjoys thinking outside the box and striving for excellence. He won a national design award from the Point of Purchasing Institute and has one U.S. Patent. However, his proudest achievement is being a father/step-father to nine children and a grandfather to eleven grandchildren.

www.ingramcontent.com/pod-product-compliance
Lightning Source LLC
Chambersburg PA
CBHW010824070526
44583CB00022B/2930